DEAF

BENEATH

Copyright © 2014, Libby Lael

DIGITAL ISBN: 978-0-578-16057-3

PAPERBACK ISBN: 978-0-578-16243-0

Thanks, Vladdi, for noticing Humanity's habitual motto:

"There's No Money In Solutions!"

DEDICATION

M. K. M., Reserve a seat for me and I'll watch you play the violin.

ACKNOWLEDGEMENTS

For Emma, the epitome of the need for LRE mandate reform. Angela D. M., the deaf drummer. Michelle Foster, my former and favorite student. David J., a force of nature. Vladdi, semi-colon dash parenthesis for the referrals, edits, and much much much more. Delta Boy and GB, for the love. And the deaf children of the public schools and the Deaf schools, without whom this book would not have been made possible.

Herb Borkland, for the novel-restructuring, mentorship and teamwork.

PREFACE

In my roles as a student and as an educator, I have witnessed for many years what few in education understand. This book reflects my experiences working just with deaf students and adults at a public elementary school that provided an inclusive deaf program. This particular inclusive public school employed faculty and staff that served as teachers both for the deaf and for the hearing, sign language interpreters, and several support staff. Before becoming employed by the public school system, I was required as part of a university classroom assignment to take a field trip to a local public school, which by happenstance directly resulted in this book.

From a cultural and linguistic perspective, I sought a common ground between the deaf students and the hearing adults, but the relationship between these deaf students and these hearing adults was oppressive at best. I struggled to raise cultural awareness and linguistic sensitivity, but I held back as I tried to keep the Individualized Education Program (IEP) on track. My attempts to maintain IEP agreement between teachers and students were met with rebuke. When it came down to dealing with educational and social inequalities among deaf students, the main motto of adults— *"It's their responsibility to listen"*— was uttered in order to silence my concerns.

As time progressed, I proposed a meeting ground between deaf students and hearing adults within the school community, because the Least Restrictive Environment mandate (LRE), a legal mandate, was not the reliable support system it claimed to be. In order to be proactive about these educational inequalities, I addressed several problematic issues, especially within the public school system and their inclusive program.

The title of this book - *Deaf Beneath* - is a term commonly used to define oppression, especially the type most often committed by audist professionals (think racist, or chauvinist; it is a belief in the superiority of hearing individuals over deaf individuals). Deaf individuals aren't supposed to be placed below normal expectations against their will, hence the wordplay of a signed phrase, "Deaf <head shake not> beneath."

For these two years, from 2003 to 2005, educational inequalities that I observed were mainly recorded as personal observations. I also recorded narrative experiences as told by adults, students and parents.

Interested readers may want to consult the Appendix for background knowledge while they delve into deeper issues surrounding deaf education programs — most notably the Least Restrictive Environment mandate, which this book is all about because it is failing the majority of the deaf students.

The journal entries in this book are inspired by true events, but names, locations, events and dates have been changed to protect the subjects' privacy.

KNIGHT ELEMENTARY SCHOOL CHARACTERS

Libby, Emma's one-on-one assistant (and this book's author)

DEAF /HARD OF HEARING STUDENTS (by age/grade level)

Blossom, Eli, Isabella, Jaber, Kayla, Rhett, Sidda, and Paxton

Michelle, Mike, Timmy, Alyssa, Emma, Joey, Dalton, and Toby

Allen, Rachel, Zeke, Stewart, Thomas, and Amanda

SIGN LANGUAGE INTERPRETERS

Brianne, Carmen, Cassie, Donna, Kallie, Pamela, Lauren, Jayme, Misty, and Cathleen, the substitute interpreter

TEACHERS FOR THE DEAF AND HARD OF HEARING STUDENTS

Mrs. Smith, pre-kindergarten

Mrs. Jones, kindergarten – second grades

Mrs. Feldman, third – fifth grades

Mrs. Miller, deaf, black, fully-qualified substitute teacher

TEACHERS FOR THE HEARING STUDENTS

Mr. Lentz and Mrs. Rickham — Second grade

Mr. Paynes and Mrs. Weaver — Third grade

Mrs. Diaz and Mrs. Taylor — Fourth grade

Mr. Bryan and Mrs. Clark — Fifth grade

Special-related teachers: Art, Gym, and Music

OTHER CHARACTERS

Ellie, sign language internship

Mr. Grant, substitute hearing teacher

Saffiyah, a deaf friend and a former student at Knight.

Leah, Eli's Mother

Brenda, Ritch's Mother

Junie, Blossom's Mother

Lisa and Chad, parents of Deaf twin sons (names unknown)

Katy, student teacher

Angela, Libby's sister

"We proceed tentatively with our words;
they soar with their signs."

Fauchet

DEAF BENEATH

PROLOGUE

Spring 2002

After a nine year break from attending Gallaudet University, I dreaded the thought of going back to school. I enrolled at a nearby university, and I sought help from my student advisor. She and I browsed university classes on the university's website so that I could sign up from her office. She informed me that a particular professor taught some of his classes in American Sign Language.

"You mean teaching ASL to the class?" I questioned.

She explained that Professor Goodman specialized in History and was also an interpreter. He occasionally switched from voice to ASL. She said that he was familiar with *Deaf Culture*, a culture that was shaped by values and norms through common perceptions, behavioral traits, and language. Values being that Deaf schools shouldn't close down, marrying another partner that's deaf, etc. Common perceptions such as that of being oppressed because the aural environment has precedence over literacy, and that deaf kids learn better in deaf-friendly and in an American Sign Language (ASL) rich environment. Behavioral traits being that deaf people typically sit with their backs to the walls in restaurants, and all these little things like that which really add up and amount to being *everything* to the deaf people.

I did not want to waste time, so I immediately signed up for one of his classes: "Deaf Studies." The idea of having ASL in the classroom appealed to me. It would be like being at Gallaudet all over again, where I received instruction in American Sign Language (ASL) in the early 90s.

1

Several weeks into the class, one of the graded assignments for the class was to pay a visit to any school that had inclusive programs for the D/HH students. Inclusive programs in public schools provided support services, sign language interpreters and teachers for the deaf students as part of the Individuals with Disabilities Education Act (IDEA) program.

The class quieted down as soon as Professor Goodman walked in the room and set his stuff down on the desk. In such a calm manner, he smiled and greeted the class in sign language and voice. Immediately, his presence showed a refinement and dignity that matched his slender physique and his signed mannerism, which was very fluid. His signing reminded me of the smoothness and strength of ballet dancing, though he himself was no dancer.

Professor Goodman explained the assignment and handed out a paper listing the schools that serviced deaf students. Looking at the list, I spotted a school that was in my hometown. The proximity between my home and the school was among the many reasons that I chose Knight Elementary School.

Knight Elementary had a program that integrated the deaf and hard of hearing students into classrooms with hearing students. As part of the IDEA program, it was school policy that the deaf students be placed in classrooms designed for hearing students at least part of (if not all of) the day.

I emailed the school for permission to visit and they approved my request, and told me my contact there would be with a Mrs. Smith.

Casually, with a map of the city in my hand, I drove around looking for the school. I finally spotted a yellow street sign that read, "Deaf Child." As I approached a four-way stop, I spotted the school on my left.

I turned and parked in front of the building, unsure of what to make of the situation. Amidst the trees scattered around the building, there was a chiseled marble sign that spelled out, "Knight Elementary School Est. 1915."

I made my way through the main entrance door. There was a large glass display case on the wall next to the cafeteria. I walked toward it and studied the pictures of the Knight staff.

On the top row were the principal, the secretary, the librarian, the nurse, and the three "special-related" activity (i.e.: art, gym and music)

2

teachers. On the second and third rows were teachers from each of the grade levels, kindergarten through fifth. Three teachers from the Deaf Education program lined the last row. These were organized from pre-kindergarten, kindergarten through second grade, and third through fifth grade. There were photos of the resource teacher, three teacher's aids, eight interpreters, four food service workers and a janitor.

I found it interesting that the deaf students' teachers were placed near the bottom rather than with their own grade levels.

From the corner of my eye, I saw a woman sitting in an office, behind a large window, motioning me to come into the air-conditioned office. The sign on her desk said, "Secretary."

After introducing myself, I asked her for directions to Mrs. Smith's classroom, and she led me on a quick walk to room 112. On the last door at the end of the hall on the right was a placard that read, "Before / After Daycare."

Mrs. Smith was a hearing teacher for the deaf pre-kindergarteners. I situated myself in her room just before class began. She explained that her classroom was converted into a daycare program in the mornings and after school hours. This infuriated her because the daycare staff and students used her school supplies. Her aggravation was understandable since deaf students are typically behind in their subjects. A daycare in her room could seriously impede the academic growth of her students if the teacher and interpreters had to spend time looking for misplaced school supplies and replacing damaged items, rather than teaching the deaf students.

I wondered why the daycare was placed in her room rather than any of the other classrooms.

Mrs. Smith had her lessons laid out for the day. All of the deaf students sat in a half circle, facing her. This half circle seating style is the best-suited method for a teacher to deliver the information to deaf students; the students could see her in order to read her lips, or to use sign language.

Mrs. Smith had one student at a time stand up, state the day, the month and his or her own name in a sentence, using the Seeing Essential English, or SEE method. At the same time, he or she was to say the sentence in the best speech possible.

3

As Mrs. Smith asked a boy to say his name. I quickly scanned his lips.

"Dibby," he said, without using sign language.

Frustrated, Mrs. Smith clutched the boy's arms, and without using sign, she said,

"No no, I need the full sentence. Copy me. My name is Timmy."

Timmy proceeded to copy the expression using sign language and not speech. Mrs. Smith gripped the child tighter and began screaming:

"You are forgetting to use your speech!"

Mrs. Smith released the boy and simultaneously signed while using voice:

"Try again."

I lip-read.

Each time one of the deaf students partook in the lesson, the student had his or her back to the other students, as they were seated in half-circle formation. Mrs. Smith probably did not realize that the deaf students could not see what their classmates were saying. Her teaching techniques were inefficient because delivering information to a deaf student at an early age is vital to his or her development.

During free play time, I reminded Mrs. Smith that the deaf students could not see her. She said that they wore their hearing aids while she was using her speech. I was unaware of that. I do not use a hearing aid, and I would have had no idea that she used her voice—except that I read her lips when I saw her mouth moving.

Later that morning, I watched two of the deaf boys, Mike and Timmy, sitting side by side, playing with toy cars. They conversed with each other fairly well—using sign language. For pre-kindergarteners, I noticed that they had the best signing skills in the class. The rest of the deaf students did not use sign language. I was intrigued with their activities, until Mrs. Smith startled me by yelling at one of them. When he did not turn to look for the source of the yelling, Mrs. Smith grabbed one of the boys by the arms, with a short jerking motion, she shouted, "You need to quiet down!"

Mrs. Smith caught me looking at her with a surprised expression.

"Deaf kids! You know how they can be when it is hard to get their attention! This one grinds his teeth and this one makes clicking noises. That bothers me." She said matter of factly.

Mrs. Smith hollered and made no attempt to conceal her message. I looked keenly at her. She was still looking at me. We stared at each other uncomfortably, not knowing what to say.

"I get headaches trying to mute them out," she said. "They are learning how to use their speech, and… you know how they sound when they don't pronounce their words clearly."

Mrs. Smith must have forgotten that I was born profoundly deaf…

Changing the subject, I asked her if the deaf students knew sign language.

"Only Mike and Timmy," she signed. "They never stop talking to each other."

Mrs. Smith went on and on about how she hated her job and was homesick for her home state. She mentioned that she was looking for someone to replace her. I told her that I knew someone who was perfect for the job.

My sister by adoption was pursuing a career in Deaf Education, after earning her Master's Degree in Deaf Education. Mrs. Smith encouraged me to have the interested person apply for the job. She grumbled that she had applied for a job in her hometown several times, but she was rejected because the school was looking for a culturally Deaf teacher. She complained that she had a right to teach at a Deaf school because she had a Master's in Special Education.

Being "culturally" Deaf means kids being brought up to deal with hearing people, and their environments as necessary, accordingly to the respective circumstantial, situational settings, such as by neighborhood, restaurants, business places, etc., and to learn various strategies to circumvent the hearing peoples' audism when encountered on a daily basis, using either or both, concurrently, the pen/paper communication methods, gestures, and/or sign language interpreters, and also how to learn to use ASL exclusively among themselves. *Non*-culturally Deaf students often do *not* know proper etiquette – like not knowing how to politely get or hold onto other deaf people's attention.

It was the perfect opportunity to ask more questions, so I asked her what the preferred method of sign language for teaching deaf students was at her home state university. She explained that she supported ASL, but the special education field at her university supported SEE 2.

After my session observing Mrs. Smith's classroom, I reported to the principal's office. The principal sported a James Van Praagh mustache, very bear-ish, and he got up from behind the desk and came around to greet me. He shook my hand, and what I hadn't noticed was that the desk had concealed a short, stout frame. I have never been considered very tall, and he stood at my eye level. I told him about my adopted sister's qualifications and he seemed very impressed.

"We have one teaching position open for deaf and hard of hearing students right now," he said with an eager grin.

I assumed that he meant Mrs. Smith's job, but he said that the vacant position was for third through fifth grades. I was confused. I thought that Mrs. Smith wanted to leave her job.

When I got home, I called my sister, Angela, on my text phone (TDD) and told her about the vacant position. She was ecstatic and asked me for the contact person.

Angela mailed her application along with her résumé and references to the school. A few days later, the principal enthusiastically wanted my sister to contact him and set up an interview. He asked me if Angela could sign. I was puzzled. Then, I realized that he did not know that Angela was also deaf. I felt it was irrelevant to inform him of my sister's deafness, so I told him that she had exceptionally great speaking and listening skills.

He shook his head and said, "No. She has to know sign language."

"Yes, she has been signing since she was about 3 years old," I added.

"Oh, that's right, for you," the principal paused awkwardly before finishing, "...because of your deafness."

A case of prejudice was happening right before my very eyes. He automatically assumed that a person with a Master's in Deaf Education must be a hearing person! He couldn't have known that Angela and I were both adopted, that one of our adoptive parents were deaf and wanted deaf children, and that they were able to provide for us as much as any other parents. Still, he assumed that she was "normal" because of her qualifications.

The principal and my sister emailed each other and eventually set up an appointment for a phone interview. He mentioned to her by email that there was a vacant teaching position for the Deaf students in the third through fifth grades.

When the interview took place, Angela called the principal via the relay service. The relay operator asked him if he knew how the relay service worked, and he replied that he didn't. The relay operator explained to him that the caller was deaf, and that the operator was equipped to handle two phone calls synchronously: one on the voice phone and the second on the text phone. The principal immediately lost interest in Angela, and told her that there were no jobs available.

During the following class at my university, I told Professor Goodman and my classmates what had taken place. The professor was not surprised. He said that he had heard of this happening repeatedly. My classmate, Jen, could not believe it. She decided to see for herself. She went to visit Mrs. Smith's classroom at a later date. Professor, my classmates and I, were all looking forward to her report so that we could compare the differences.

Jen showed up at the next class with a big grin on her face. She wanted us to wait until all of the students arrived before she told us what happened.

As soon as Professor Goodman walked in and placed his notes on his desk, Jen told us what she experienced at the school. Jen was in Mrs. Smith's class, watching Mrs. Smith yell at the deaf students to use their voices. Jen narrated her experience in sign language:

"Voice!"

"Where's your voice!"

"I don't hear your voice!"

Jen said, "While staying there, I clenched my jaws. I wished that I could stop this, but I was there only to observe.

"Later in the day, Mike stood by the toy stove and made a loud 'zzzz' sound, as if his hamburger was sizzling in the hot pan. Mrs. Smith yelled at Mike to shut up. It startled me from where I was sitting!"

Deaf children have no clear understanding of the difference between producing sounds and silence. He may have felt the vibration of sound in his throat, but he would have to struggle to hear or understand his own voice. How do you shut up a deaf child, if he only has a vague understanding of what sound is? Mrs. Smith wanted the Deaf children to use their voices at times, but at other times she did not want them to use their voices. Deaf students do not know the difference between when it is appropriate to use their voices and when it isn't.

Jen continued, "Intermittently, over the course of the observation, Mrs. Smith offered me her job several times. I was shocked. I am only a sophomore, and not even into the Education major yet!"

Surprised at Mrs. Smith's bias, I asked Jen what she had that I lacked. Professor Goodman and the rest of the class looked on contemplatively as Jen replied:

"Hearing status."

Knight School was very hearing oriented. Their preferred method of instruction was orally, and the teachers for the D/HH students resorted to using SEE when it was necessary to clarify the communication.

"But it is a waste of time to try and speak orally to deaf students, only to find that they did not understand what you said," Professor Goodman signed. "Then, you have to sign the same message again, just to deliver the point that could have easily been signed the first time."

"Precisely," Jen signed.

All the others in the room nodded.

One of my classmates asked me a perturbing question:

"Do all deaf students have behavior problems?"

"No…they fidget, that's all," I replied. I decided to ask her, "What makes you think that deaf students have behavior problems?"

"My hearing professor, who teaches a course in special education for the Education major program, said that all deaf children have problems with behavior," she signed slowly to deliver her message perfectly signed.

Seething, I signed slowly so that the hearing students could read my signs:

"This is a huge misconception. The main reason that deaf children are labeled with behavior problems is because of communication issues. Most of them lack satisfying communication at home. So they go feral. Just like that feral girl, Genie Wiley, who we learned about the other week."

During the following class, we had a guest speaker from the university hospital. She specialized in recruiting parents to consider embedding Cochlear Implants (CI) into their deaf children. The guest spoke about the mechanism of the CI device, the total costs, the risks relating to the surgery, and the aftermaths of therapies relating to CI. (She did not mention the thousands of frustrating hours of therapy, the loss of identity for the child, the necessity of permanently erasing the child's residual hearing, or the risk of death.)

Just as the speaker ended her presentation, she emphasized that the deaf recipients of CI are not allowed on the plastic slides. She said that the static, resulting from sliding down the plastic, can damage the device. When the CI breaks, the parents must bring it to the university's Speech Pathology department to have it fixed. The CI child would be left without the device for several days. The only back up is the behind the ear (BTE) hearing aid, which can only be used in the ear that was not implanted.

I thought, "What happens if the backup hearing devices are not an affordable option?"

Nearing the end of the period, the speaker asked the class if we had any more questions or comments. Wanting to be the first person to make a comment, I raised my hand. Professor Goodman quickly switched to the role of interpreter, using his voice as he interpreted my question.

"What did you mean when you said that the deaf recipients are not allowed to play on plastic slides? Can't they take the CI off and go on the slides? To limit a child from playing on a slide really says a lot."

The guest speaker defensively responded that the static lingers on the child's clothes. When the child puts the CI back on, the lingering static breaks the CI, and the child cannot use it to hear.

Jen pointed out to the guest speaker, using sign language (which was the classroom policy), that the deaf child would then have no way to communicate with his or her parents, because most hearing parents of deaf children do not learn to sign. In a way, they still think their child is instantly a hearing person.

We watched the guest speaker squirm, trying to present a convincing point. She said that the university hospital provides counseling, guidance and a support system; in fact, it was one of the few universities that supported dual communication, using both speech and sign language. She smiled triumphantly.

Before the class ended, Jen jumped in, "With or without the CI, the implanted child is still *legally* deaf..."

> "One can never consent to creep when
> one feels the impulse to soar."
>
> *Helen Keller*

FIRST SEASON

Saturday, September 6, 2003 (a year later)

I had been looking for job opportunities closer to home, when one Saturday, I took my foster children to a local city park. A woman came and joined me on the park bench where I sat watching my children play.

My kids came running up to me signing and then ran back to play some more. The woman next to me waved into my peripheral vision and introduced herself in sign language. At first I thought she was mocking me because she did not move her hands fluently. Her movements reminded me of two fish flopping around on dry land, gasping for air. It is probably like listening to an alcoholic's hoarse voice mumbling.

After I got used to her hand movements, the woman introduced herself as Carmen. Carmen was an unusual woman with distracting features. Her teeth reminded me of little yellow pegs scattered about in her mouth, with dark brown dots littered across her gum lines, evidencing years and years of caffeine and tobacco abuse. Her breath reeked of the rancid, acidic smell of stale coffee and cigarettes.

Still, at the time, she seemed nice enough. Carmen said that she was an interpreter for the deaf at Knight School. After some small talk, she told me that there was a job available at Knight for a teacher's aide, working with a developmentally challenged deaf student.

"That is what the itinerant teacher for the deaf from the Area Education Agency (AEA) told me. She said that a deaf girl from a rural farming community was transferred here," I said.

Carmen asked me what the girl's name was, adding "I think I know who you are talking about."

"Emma, I think," I replied.

11

Carmen nodded and signed rather awkwardly, "Most definitely, Emma. I was talking about the available job... that job is to work with her."

I still couldn't shake what had happened between my sister and the principal over a year earlier. However, I needed a job, and this seemed promising. Restless, yet patient, I waited until the following Monday morning and hurried to the local school board's human resource office to apply for the job. Several email correspondences confirmed my appointment for an interview.

Tuesday, September 9

I walked into the school office and spoke to the secretary in my best, but often unintelligible, 'deaf speech.'

"My name is Libby. I'm here for the interview," I said.

The secretary told me to wait in the lobby.

I walked over to the glass display to look at the new faces. The D/HH teachers were still positioned near the bottom of the display.

Five minutes later, two interviewers greeted me and led me into the office. They introduced themselves as the principal and Mrs. Jones, who taught the deaf students from kindergarten to second grade. After the interview, they hired me on the spot, as a one-on-one aide to a developmentally challenged deaf girl in the second grade.

Mrs. Jones provided a tour and an orientation, two weeks before I was scheduled to begin work. Classes for the semester had already begun.

In Mrs. Jones' room, there were six individual desks, split up into two groups, based on grade levels. They were placed across from each other, with three trapezoid tables neatly arranged in the middle of the room, in a semi-circle, separating them. Two computer desks were set against the blackboard on the right side of the room, and two adult desks were in the far left corner, near the adult bathroom. The adult desks were for the interpreters and Mrs. Jones.

The second bathroom was at the opposite corner, obscured by a portable partition wall. There was an independent play center and a lot of books near the doorway. Next to that was a wooden credenza, where the deaf students gathered to change their hearing aids, replace their batteries and put on assistive listening devices. Several microphones were plugged into the station.

Mrs. Jones showed me how to put the auditory training devices on the student's hearing aids. She emphasized that the trainers were very expensive. Most of the students wore two hearing aids, except for Joey and Timmy.

Mrs. Jones reminded one of the boys that he forgot to put on his trainers. She signed using Exact English: "Train (as in a locomotive train) + R + S," ending the word with the manual alphabet.

Confused, I asked her what the trainers were for. She clarified and said, "Trainers are also called auditory trainers, boots, boot trainers, FM, micro links or links, whichever suits you."

She did not answer my question, and it took me a while to figure out what they were. After seeing the deaf students talk into their assigned microphones, while adjusting the trainers on their hearing aids, it dawned on me that they were similar to what I had when I was a young student, only smaller, and the colors were a bland shade of gray. Trainers enabled the teachers to deliver spoken messages directly to the student's hearing aid.

The confusion for students between using sign language and the dependency of wearing the trainers was detrimental, but the deaf students often seemed helpless without them, because they could not keep their eyes on the teacher due to external noises.

Using the trainers also wasted time—the students had to fiddle with them to make sure they were working properly. Since most of the students had been mainstreamed for a long time, it made sense to keep them aurally hooked until they could acquire a deaf lifestyle through American Sign Language. It wouldn't be a good idea if the trainers or listening devices were taken from them, especially while they still lacked language and cultural identity as to whether to use sign language and be reprimanded or be like *them* and totally miss out on a lot, in an aural rich environment over the visual rich environment.

Immediately after the orientation, Mrs. Jones gave me a list of the deaf students and interpreters, and she told me to memorize their names and grade levels.

Jayme and Cassie were interpreters for Mrs. Smith's pre-kindergarten class: Blossom, Eli, Isabella, Jaber, Kayla, Rhett and Sidda.

Donna, Pamela and Brianne were interpreters for Mrs. Jones' kindergarten through second grade class: Michelle, Mike, Timmy, Alyssa, Emma, Dalton, Joey and Toby.

Carmen and Lauren were interpreters for Mrs. Feldman's third through fifth grade class: Allen, Rachel, Zeke, Stewart, Thomas and Amanda.

Wednesday, September 24

Two weeks later, on my way to Mrs. Jones' classroom, I walked by Mrs. Smith's classroom and witnessed the same outbursts that I'd seen a year and a half earlier. There was a new placard above the old one: "Teacher's Lounge," and "Before / After Daycare." I couldn't help but wonder what had happened since I was here last.

About 25 paces down the hall was the door to Mrs. Jones' classroom. I stepped in and began my first day of work.

There were the eight deaf students, five boys and three girls: Michelle, Mike, Timmy, Alyssa, Emma, Dalton, Joey and Toby. Mrs. Jones introduced me to the three full-time interpreters who worked directly with the deaf children.

Donna interpreted for a kindergartener named Michelle. Pamela interpreted for two first graders, Mike and Timmy. Brianne interpreted for the five second graders, Alyssa, Emma, Dalton, Joey and Toby. The interpreters switched around when needed.

That morning the interpreters went about their business—checking emails, paying for their school lunches, and eating breakfast from the school cafeteria—before starting their work. I sat by the interpreter's desk, trying to settle in. I quietly observed the deaf students and the interpreters interacting with the adult staff, who seemed to frequently pop in and out of the classroom. I patiently waited for the day to begin at 9:10.

Mrs. Jones approached me and said that the deaf second graders (except for Emma) went upstairs to Mr. Lentz's classroom for most of the day, to be integrated with the hearing students. She handed me the daily schedule and told me to study it.

The schedule looked simple enough, but it had a lot of interruptions.

Pamela, one of the interpreters, walked over to the desk where I sat. I asked her why the school switched Mrs. Smith's former room. Pamela, being accustomed to signing for young deaf students who do not have a strong language foundation, slowly signed that Mrs. Smith's classroom was transferred to an annex trailer, and the daycare room was converted into the teacher's lounge during the day.

Back in 2002, the third through fifth grade D/HH room was right next to the teacher's lounge on the second floor. It was a very small room. Yet, this year, Mrs. Feldman's D/HH classroom had been transferred into the teacher's lounge despite her objections.

The current classroom was small, about the size of a child's bedroom. I checked it out, and it was large enough for one twin sized mattress, two nightstands and a bureau drawer. The room was cramped with five student desks, two adult desks and seven people.

Mrs. Feldman's former classroom was given to the resource room teacher for 25 hearing students who had learning disabilities. They came in at different times during the day. The deaf students had needed that room in order to have some elbow room to sign naturally. Now they were packed in like canned sardines.

This inclusive program truly minimized Deaf education. It disregarded the deaf program and gave the hearing classes the educational advantage.

Mrs. Jones walked over to the light switch and flicked the lights off and on to notify the deaf students that it was time to stop their free time and clean up. I got up from where I sat at the desk and walked over to help the deaf students, when Alyssa waved to get my attention. Alyssa's eyes darted between Joey and me. As soon as Joey looked at Alyssa, she pointed her finger at me and spoke unintelligibly.

"BB new bool," she signed the first two words to Joey.

What did she just say? I wondered.

15

Joey ignored Alyssa by breaking eye contact and kept playing with his dominoes.

Maintaining eye contact is an essential part of American Sign Language, a *must* skill in the Deaf community. Breaking eye contact equals ending the communication in a very rude tone. Naturally, Joey did not know any better. This is a common problem among mainstreamed deaf children of hearing parents, who have no cultural identity. More specifically, it is common with schools that do not incorporate Deaf culture into their curriculum. Deaf students need constant exposure to the Deaf culture. This school brought in a Deaf person once a month for a 'touch based storytelling,' which was unfortunately not sufficient to provide enough exposure to the deaf children in a timely manner.

"There is not one shred of social skills going on here," I thought to myself. I decided to explain to Joey that it was polite to look at Alyssa while she was signing. Joey ignored me, so I asked him to clean up for community circle time.

During the group circle time, I brainstormed all the possibilities of what "BB new bool" meant. I lip-synced Alyssa's mouth movements, two syllables for "BB." I knew her sign for "New," so I moved on to the next sign that contained a puff with the ending "L" which placed the tongue behind the top teeth for the supposed word, "Bool." After playing with the letters and the words like a jigsaw puzzle, a light bulb went off in my head. It dawned on me that Alyssa had said, "Libby new school," which probably meant that I was new to the school.

My attention was diverted to Timmy who was complaining to his teacher that his stepfather had thrown away his monthly sign-in reading sheet. Timmy continued to complain because he wanted to be able to take home free books from the classroom.

After circle time, the students had a chance to play with the hand coordination toys for a while. I did not know how the take home reading sheet worked and this was a good time to ask Mrs. Jones about it.

Mrs. Jones explained to me that the parents were to fill in the titles of the books that their children read at home in order for the deaf students to get a free book to take home each month.

Obviously, Timmy's stepfather was willing to sacrifice this opportunity for free books, taking away Timmy's chances of bettering his English skills. Reading, writing and comprehension are the fundamental cores that free deaf people from being dependent on hearing people. Good reading skills enable deaf people to use TDD, text pagers, write notes to hearing people, and to read closed captioning on media programs. Higher literacy empowers deaf people's independence.

Not all deaf people can speak well or lip read. However, speaking and lip reading (or the lack of it) does not affect a person's intelligence. Effective communication leads to comprehension, and comprehending the context of a printed message is a sign of good literacy skills.

Brianne sat with me and explained Toby, Joey and Dalton's behavior. I was repeatedly cautioned that all three boys fought and competed endlessly with one another for friendship. Toby would pit Dalton against Joey and Joey would push Dalton's buttons. All of the children had their own peculiarities.

Toby, a tall blue-eyed brunette was into his second year at Knight and his literacy skills were of serious concern. He was diagnosed with a mild hearing loss just a year before, post-lingually deaf. He had acquired speaking skills before his hearing had deteriorated and he just started learning sign language.

However, Toby was able to wear a hearing aid without any further intervention because the school provided a tele-loop listening device. The listening device was equipped with three parts: the headphones, the cord and the processor. This tele-loop was to help amplify the sounds while blocking out background noises. Toby said that the device did not work half the time, but he also found ways to avoid wearing the tele-loop device.

A plus about Toby is that he was extremely conniving—sneaky, but in a good way—finding ways to get around his literacy disabilities. Simply put, he was a nice kid who knew how to get away with it.

Dalton was a kid with enormous brown eyes and even darker hair. He exerted a domineering presence in the classroom and on the playground. His hearing loss was moderate, but he had excellent speech skills. In spite of his advantage, he had an underlying behavior management problem. I attributed this to the lack of communication with him at home; his father lacked patience and didn't use sign language. Dalton had a mild reading and writing deficiency, but not as low as Toby. One of Dalton's best qualities was his acting abilities.

Dalton and Toby were both behind in their reading skills. On the other hand, Joey was ahead of all the other deaf second graders, and his academic level was on target with his hearing peers. Joey's main problem was his inability to listen and follow directions.

Except for Michelle and Mike, Joey was smaller than the rest of his peers, an elfin-like blonde. His world revolved around him. It was clear from the statements he made that his parents fostered this 'Me' complex in him by bragging that his CI was the best and that all the other hearing aids were for 'dumb kids'. So he said.

Brianne explained that Joey did not want to be identified as a deaf child, so he often refused to use sign language. His mother magnified his deafness into something of a pathological issue. Yet, Joey was the loneliest among his deaf peers. He did not know which group to call his own.

Joey and Timmy both had CIs. Joey's CI, however, was far superior to Timmy's. It looked sparkly new, as if it had just come out of the box. The removable pieces were fashionable and interchangeable. His CI processor was the size of a cigarette lighter and hung precariously behind his ear. It always looked as if it were going to fall off.

Timmy's CI appeared to be worn out. The rubbery cord that encased the wires, which connect the magnetic earpiece to the machine that processes and transmits the sounds, was peeling apart, exposing the wires. The magnetic part inside the ear had dirt smeared on it. His CI was strapped in a frayed case suspended from his belt.

The boys' parents couldn't have been more different. Joey frequented a deaf camp in the Rockies for kids with cochlear implants. Timmy lacked such privileges. Joey's parents signed, while Timmy's stepfather did not sign and his mother did so clumsily. I could tell right away that they came from different socioeconomic backgrounds.

Mrs. Jones took the time to explain to me about the rest of the deaf children. Mike wore two "behind the ear" (BTE) hearing aids, and had near perfect speech – but his parents argued frequently, and the mother particularly had caved into Mike's tendencies to use sign language and leaving hearing aids lying around. Alyssa had a hard of hearing father who was also a former student of Mrs. Jones', and she was deficient in her expressive skills. Emma was enrolled just this year and she was a deaf child with multi-disabilities. Her home school could not help to pull up her literacy level because of her behavior problems. Emma's home school program did not allow Emma to take the naps that were required by her Individualized Education Program (IEP) agreement. Just recently, the Knight school officials decided to take Emma out of the hearing classrooms, except for special-related lessons.

Mike and Timmy were inseparable. They tended to disregard their assignments to talk endlessly with each other. Perhaps it was because they were the only deaf children at their grade level, or maybe it was because they had been classmates with each other since pre-kindergarten. Or a little of both.

As for Michelle, this kindergarten student, a mute, was very analytical and quite brilliant. She wore two BTEs and had just started learning sign language. She disliked changes in her daily routine and this created problems with anyone who worked with her. Any changes in the future had to be introduced to her before an actual change took place, such as new or substitute D/HH staff. Trust had to be earned with this child.

After Mrs. Jones finished detailing each student's background, I told her that I knew Mike from a local Deaf Club. Mike had a best friend named Ritch. Ritch was the deaf child of a Deaf father and hearing mother, Brenda. They were also family friends of mine.

I recounted a story that Ritch's mother told me.

"Her son was at a local parade hosted by the university that I attended. People on the floats threw bagels into the crowd and one hit Ritch in the head. Brenda picked it up and showed it to Ritch. She explained to him that people ate bagels with cream cheese. She manually spelled out the word, 'B-A-G-E-L.'

"The following school day, Ritch sat in his first grade classroom, one city away from Knight Elementary. Ritch's hearing teacher was teaching the class about food groups and the food pyramid. Ritch, being the only Deaf child in the classroom, relied on an interpreter who knew nothing about Deaf culture. The interpreter did not know ASL.

"The teacher flashed cards with pictures of the different foods. A picture of a bagel came up and Ritch signed excitedly with one hand, pointing to the picture with the other, 'I saw yesterday!'

"The interpreter translated verbally, 'I saw you yesterday.' The teacher looked at Ritch in confusion and said, 'Where?'

The interpreter looked at Ritch and signed 'Where?'

Ritch signed (still pointing at the picture) 'I saw parade yesterday.'

The interpreter looked at the teacher and signed, 'I saw you at the parade yesterday.'

The teacher became upset and said, 'I was not at the parade yesterday!'" Miscommunication ensued.

Ritch continued to defend his point until he, the teacher and the interpreter began to argue. Ritch was sent out to sit in the hallway.

I thought to myself, Ritch must have forgotten the word 'bagel' because he continued to point at the picture.

It's this ... or Ritch used his index finger to identify or connect to the picture of a bagel. Indexing is widely used for pronouns in ASL. This action of indexing is also known as pronominalization, a principle of using pronouns in a basic sense. Ritch showed relevance by pointing to the bagel in the picture while simultaneously talking about seeing such a bagel at the parade.

The parents were not to be blamed. The school refused to hire an ASL interpreter because SEE 2 was widely enforced and heavily favored. Scapegoating the teacher for allowing the miscommunication to happen would have been easy enough, but it wasn't the teacher. The school's policy was to blame. An educated and certified interpreter probably would have interrupted Ritch and asked for clarification.

Thursday, September 25

The following morning, I stood by the doorway chatting with Lauren in sign language. She leaned over and called to Carmen to stop and come in. She asked Carmen how the word 'office' was signed. Carmen eagerly signed the word for 'organization' using ASL, while she simultaneously mouthed the word, 'office.'

I tried to explain to Carmen that she signed the ASL word incorrectly. "The sign you used means 'organization' in ASL…"

Just as I started to demonstrate the correct sign for 'office,' Lauren interrupted me and defensively said, "She has more signing experience than you, and I would recommend that you go and look up the words 'organization' and 'office' in the Signing Exact English handbook. You know, that thick yellow book!"

If Carmen had actually been using SEE 2, the word would have been signed completely differently, and Lauren would have picked up on this mistake. In SEE 2, Carmen would have used the manual suffix 'ion' for the word 'organization'.

Offended by the insult, I shot back, "Interpreter Lauren, I have been signing for all my life and ASL is my native language. Do not tell me to look it up in the Signing Exact English book. I suggest that you look it up. It does not make sense to say, 'Let's go to the organization and office the flyers into stacks of color groups!'"

Both Carmen and Lauren left.

Donna came up and said, "I saw what happened. I'm sorry that it happened to you. I don't know what Lauren was thinking."

Donna and I scurried to the back of the room and looked up the words 'office' and 'organization' in the infamous mega-book, "Signing Exact English." The signs in the book confirmed that I had been right the whole time.

Donna tapped me on the shoulder to get my attention and said, "I've heard that the interpreter should not criticize a deaf person's sign language."

"Yes. It would be like me, a profoundly deaf person, criticizing a hearing person's speech," I replied.

21

Later that morning, we were getting the deaf students ready for lunch. I asked Emma to wash her hands. Emma refused, and Mrs. Jones looked busy, so I decided to pull a behavior management trick.

"Your hands are very filthy. They've been in everything, so you need to wash them. You may not have your lunch until you wash your hands," I said.

Emma put her hands behind her back and shoved them down into her pants. I thought she was restraining herself, but she instantly took out a darkened hand and tried to touch my face.

The offending odor wafted by my nose. I grabbed her by the wrist and saw the poop on her hands. While I was busy wrestling her hand away from my face, she nearly got me with her other hand.

I admonished her, "If you do not stop, there will be no recess for you today!"

Emma smiled coyly and said, "Lick."

"No!" I screamed in panic, while restraining both of her hands from touching my face.

She yanked her hands from my grip and licked the brown substance from her hands. Mrs. Jones saw the incident and told me to take her to the bathroom and block the door until she came out squeaky clean.

Emma quickly acted appropriately from then on.

Still shaken by the incident with Emma, I was escorted to the teacher's lounge by Mrs. Jones and Donna for our lunch break. Mrs. Jones interpreted some of the teachers' conversation. I learned that a Parent Teacher Association (PTA) leader wanted to preserve the big teachers' lounge. The PTA wanted to combine all the deaf students, from pre-k to fifth grade, into one classroom setting. If that were to happen, the constant rotation of students coming and going would cause a chaotic learning environment.

I was surprised, but I did not want to seem reactionary, so I digressed. I asked Mrs. Jones how I should have handled Emma better.

Mrs. Jones put her sandwich down and replied:

"You'll need to devise a behavior management plan if she continues these kinds of inappropriate outbursts."

Listening intently, I nodded and wanted to know more:

"Is she always like this?"

Mrs. Jones explained further:

"Yes, sometimes worse. Her needs took my attention away from the other deaf students. That's not fair to them and that is why we hired you. She used to go to Mr. Lentz's room, but Brianne couldn't control Emma's behavior and interpret for the class at the same time. We withdrew her from most of Mr. Lentz's classes except for the special-related classes."

"What are special-related classes," I asked.

"Music, art, gym, library and computer lab," Mrs. Jones replied.

Monday, September 29

Right after I walked into the classroom, Mrs. Jones told me to expect a visit from a university student that afternoon. The student wanted to interview me about my work. I realized the importance of making this issue known, especially to a hearing student.

To my surprise, the student used sign language.

"Why do you feel that you, with your disability, are appropriate for the classroom setting, either in a regular classroom, or in a D/HH program?" she asked.

"The deaf children are consistently amazed to see a deaf person in their class. They ask me the kinds of questions that they would never ask a hearing adult. I feel that is important because a lot of deaf children have the misbeliefs that they will either become hearing, or die, when they grow up...probably due to the fact that they never get to see deaf adults. This, of course, does not apply to children with deaf parents."

"How do co-workers react when they realize that you are hearing impaired?"

"They do not ask me questions directly or initiate conversations with me. They usually find more about me only after I actively approach them.

23

"This is rather a typical thing. For instance, they often tell the hearing signers what they want to tell me, rather than talking with me directly.

"They usually say, 'Tell Libby…' whatever it is that they want me to know, all of this while I'm not even in the same room. They exclude me from my own conversation. This is a huge turn off, but I understand that they do not know how to interact appropriately with deaf people. The best method is to use pen and paper to communicate with me."

"What are some positive first time interactions with others…specifically with teachers, principals, parents and students?"

"Oh gee, the art teacher is great! He does not go to the interpreters to try and talk to me. He patiently tries to carry a conversation with me and he takes the time to understand my speech. We have a great understanding with each other. The parents of the deaf students usually understand me, just like the art teacher. I wish there were more people like him.

"One mom has a kid with a cochlear implant. She is not so crazy about me because I do not wear hearing aids. I think she is concerned that I might influence her kid with my reasons for not wearing them. I'm totally deaf for one."

"What are some negative first time interactions with others, specifically with teachers, students, principals and parents?"

"Oh… mostly disbelief… just by the looks on their faces. I cannot speak for others. Nearly none of them understand Deaf culture anyway.

"Mrs. Jones even hinted to me that it would be better financially if I were hearing, because then I could perform dual functions as an interpreter and a teacher's aide. If one or more of the interpreters were out sick, I could act as an interpreter. As a Deaf person, I am unable to do that, the interpreting part."

During my lunch break in the teacher's lounge, Mrs. Feldman introduced me to a tall black woman, Mrs. Miller. Mrs. Feldman told me that she is the preferred substitute teacher for the deaf students, because of her ability to transcend all the communication levels: reading, writing, speaking and signing.

Mrs. Miller signed to me, and we hit it off right away because of what we had in common. We were both deaf. She moved around the teacher's lounge with confident laughter. Her charisma was captivating.

"We're gonna be friends," I thought to myself.

Wednesday, October 8

It was a crisp autumn morning. I walked into the classroom and saw the interpreters rearranging the student's desks.

"What's going on?" I asked.

One of the interpreters stopped what she was doing and explained, "The students are having Student Aptitude Test (SAT) assessment tests today. We want them to sit separately."

The principal said that the Diagnostic Reading Assessments were limited to 24 minutes per segment. Mrs. Jones disregarded the principal's comments and allowed the deaf students to have 50 minutes per segment.

The first group to take the test was the first and second graders.

Mrs. Jones asked me to help the deaf students settle down and prepare for the test. I noticed that neither the SAT-9 nor the SAT-Hearing impaired versions were being used. I asked Mrs. Jones about this.

"This school district chooses not to use those," she replied. "I just skip the phonetics part, which isn't a problem."

To my right, Brianne was sitting with one of the students. I asked Mrs. Jones what she was doing.

"She's helping me with the assessment because I am behind on the report cards," Mrs. Jones replied.

Mrs. Jones' comment piqued my attention, so I offered to help by assessing one of the students for them. The women told me that I could not do the job because part of the assessment was counting the words of the students.

Perplexed, I asked audibly, "What about them using sign language instead?"

I was met with stern disapproval. Mrs. Jones explained to me that it took longer to use signs because the students did not know sign language very well. This was definitely a fact. Yet, what if a deaf student did not understand a particular word, but pronounced it correctly? It would be counted and marked down.

For instance, the commonly misspelled words, 'Meat' and 'Meet' have different meanings. There are different signs for those particular words. What if the deaf student confused the meaning of the two words? Sometimes it is better for them to sign the word to make sure that the listener understands fully what they mean. When assessing for comprehension, then responses that clearly show comprehension are far more important than how fast or how well a deaf student can speak during an assessment.

Over the course of the day, the interpreters argued their opinions about whether interpreters and teachers' aides should be included in the IEP meetings with parents. Lauren and Carmen argued fervently. That afternoon, the D/HH teachers and several of the interpreters asked my opinion about the matter.

I was opposed to having teachers' aides and interpreters at the meetings. Lauren, Carmen, and a teacher I would come to dislike, named Mrs. Weaver, all disagreed and sent an email to the principal, asking that the interpreters be included on the IEP team. The D/HH teachers supported my position because there were already so many people involved in the IEP process as it was. The principal sent an email to the staff, explaining the protocols.

From the Deaf perspective, whether or not the teachers' aides and interpreters participated within the scope of the IEP was not the problem. The main problem was in the method used by the D/HH teachers and interpreters to communicate with the students. They currently used Signed Exact English 2 (SEE2), which was confusing to the students at best. American Sign Language is the natural language for deaf children to communicate with, just as speech is the natural language for hearing children to use.

I emailed the principal and explained to him that SEE is confusing because of its misuse of morphemes (a "morpheme" is a minimum component of a meaningful word) in sign language. The D/HH teachers may use the signs appropriately, but semantically, the signs have different meanings. However, he replied back stating that he trusts the D/HH teachers and staff.

The D/HH teachers and just about everyone else, especially the school based interpreters, did not execute proper use of SEE 2. Worse, they did not even understand the long term effects that using incorrect signs would have on these students: SEE 1 is a method of signing each morpheme while verbally speaking the word. Each written or spoken morpheme has a certain placement in the word and the sentence, but signed morphemes do not fit into the same grammatically correct sentence structure.

One example of this is the word 'Also.' The word 'Also' is one word, with one definition. It is an adverb that means 'Too'. However, the inexperienced SEE 2 signer might separate the word 'Also' into two signs, 'All,' and 'So,' giving the word a completely different meaning. The word 'All' means 'Every' or 'Total' and the word 'So' means 'Thus.' It is the English equivalent of saying, "We every thus (all + so) have to go."

This is confusing to experienced signers, and it is even more-so to children still learning vocabulary.

This gets complicated further when you consider the meanings of the words 'All' and 'So'. In ASL, there are different signs for the word 'All', depending on its use as an adjective, adverb or pronoun. In SEE 2, the signed word 'All' means the whole amount or quantity in the adjective sense. Yet, the SEE 2 signer may use the same word in the adverb sense, as in "Played all alone." This is often used as an intensive word, rather than the sign to represent the adjective or pronoun. The word 'All' used as a pronoun indicates the whole group or amount. The word 'So' can be an adverb indicating greater or larger, or "So" can be a conjunction meaning 'Thus'.

When people speak these homonyms aloud, the pronunciation remains the same and the hearing listener doesn't know the difference. Deaf people cannot hear the pronunciation of the word, and they must rely solely on the grammar and syntax of the sentence to discern meaning, a feat that is confusing or impossible for inexperienced young signers. ASL was designed with this in mind. It allows the deaf listener to easily discern the grammar and syntax differences by using different signs to indicate the different meanings of the same word.

Students learning to sign using SEE must quickly learn English grammar and syntax, or they will fall very far behind their classmates in comprehension. Students learning to sign using ASL are able to learn comprehension much more quickly, giving them better opportunities to keep up with their hearing counterparts.

These students will be greatly misunderstood by the Deaf community (the hearing community, for the most part, does not sign at all). Typically, they will be treated as outcasts if they continue to use these incorrect signs.

Monday, October 13

It was a cool Monday morning. I found a note on my desk that said, "I'm in a meeting. Please welcome Ellie to the class and help her to navigate her way around the school. She's a student interpreter from the local community college and will be with us during her practicum.

– Mrs. Jones – "

A few minutes later, Ellie showed up looking very unprofessional. Her hair style was that of a mall–addicted teen and she had caked on makeup plastered all over her face. She wore an extremely short mini-skirt and carried a ton of books, a tote bag and two thermoses in her arms.

I have noticed that the more educated the interpreters were, the more knowledgeable about the subjects, the better they seemed to dress. Ellie at the time did not seem very impressive.

I showed Ellie where she could put her belongings and explained to her how busy it could get. There might be no leisure time to read novels. I took out the classroom photo album and showed Ellie the pictures of the deaf students so that she could learn their names.

Mrs. Jones returned and informed me and Ellie that Brianne would be in Mr. Lentz's classroom and that Ellie would be interpreting. For Ellie to interpret without professional observation was strictly against her practicum where she was supposed to be observing interpreters and/to interpret (under observation) as well. Ellie was supposed to have an observer to give her constructive critique.

When it was time to take the students downstairs to the gym class, I had Ellie shadow me so that she could learn the layout of the school. Ellie and I stood in line with the deaf and hearing students waiting to be called into the gym. Toby started to crowd the hearing students in front of him because he saw bowling sets on the gym floor. The hearing students behind Toby heard about the bowling pins and rubber balls, so they crowded Toby from behind, trying to see around him.

Ellie stood near the door and focused on Toby. With arched eyebrows, and pursed lips she ordered him to get back in line. Toby tried to do what he was told, but the other students were crowding him in. After the third warning, Ellie grabbed Toby by the arm and sent him to the back of the queue.

She seemed to be selectively biased toward Toby for some reason and I needed to create a diversion to break her attention away from him.

I yelled at Ellie and using larger spatial signs than normal I said, "If you told him to go to the back of the line, you should tell all of the students blocking the doorway to go to the back of the line too."

It was not fair that she picked only on the deaf students; they were already being constantly dissected under a magnifying glass.

Nonetheless, by the end of the day, Ellie began to understand what I had meant. Hopefully she would learn by the time she left us.

Monday, October 20

The second grade deaf students had computer lab with Mr. Lentz's class. Ellie stood in the back of the room reading the infamous "Signing Exact English" handbook. "That book needs to be burned," I thought to myself.

Alyssa waved to get my attention and showed me something on her computer monitor.

"Store Mama Poppa Shoes CC Store." It was her best typed sentence.

"Mama what?" I asked her using my simplest sign language.

Alyssa pointed to her shoes and fingerspelled, "C-C."

I asked her again, "C-C what?"

She signed slower, "C-C Halloween."

After brainstorming, I finally figured it out. "Oh! You mean Cinderella costume! What about the shoes?"

She replied in the same unintelligible format.

I tried to clarify what she meant by echoing her comment, "Mama and Poppa went to the store and bought a Cinderella costume and a pair of new shoes, right?"

She nodded in affirmation.

From the corner of my eye, I noticed that Ellie had observed the conversation between Alyssa and me. I got up and walked over to check the other deaf student's work, when Ellie approached me. She asked me what was wrong with Alyssa.

Without going into great detail, I explained that most deaf students have a below normal reading and writing level. Ellie's face contorted in a pained expression, as if to imply that deaf students are below average intelligence as well.

I continued, "No, it isn't what you think."

Ellie's face morphed into a sad puppy-eyed gaze and she placed her hands over her heart.

I left her standing there and resumed my tasks.

Friday, October 24

Why are the deaf students required to take music classes is beyond me, but I dismissed that thought as I led Ellie and the deaf second graders to their music class for that day's lessons. We waited for the hearing second graders to come in before the lesson started. Brianne escorted the hearing second graders to the music class rather than let Mr. Lentz do it himself.

Taking students to the special-related class was the teacher's job, but the teachers at Knight Elementary knew how to take full advantage of the interpreters. They were over-worked because of the close proximity with the deaf students all day.

The music teacher greeted us as we walked into the classroom, which was tiny and crowded with 25 electronic keyboards. She got up from the floor clutching notebooks close to her chest, and then she walked over to the front of the room in quite a prim and proper gait, not moving her head much. She towered above most of the adults, but she didn't bring attention to herself, as she remained expressionless most of the time. She only moved her arms when necessary, and she did not speak much. Her lips were unreadable as they were razor thin and remained motionless, like a ventriloquist.

The music teacher explained to the class that this was the first time that the electronic keyboards were introduced to the music program. I observed the interpreting setting and realized that the keyboards were set so high on the desks that they blocked the students' view of the interpreters. I asked the deaf students to sit together so that they could see Brianne better.

Brianne interrupted me.

"The music teacher assigned seats to each child. They need to stay there for the duration of this electronic keyboard program."

"Some of the deaf students cannot see you, the other students, or even the teacher," I quietly signed.

Ellie looked lost and helpless, agreeing with me as I tried to explain the purpose of helping the deaf students see the interpreter from a better angle.

"Well, they know that they are supposed to be able to see either the music teacher, or me. They just need to listen." Brianne replied.

"Either?" I thought to myself.

They were supposed to be able to see both of the adults, not just one or the other. With this seating arrangement, they couldn't even see their own deaf friends. They were supposed to be able to see all of the adults, all of the visual displays, and their friends. That is required by the "Least Restrictive Environment" clause. It is not a least restrictive environment if they do not have as equal access as their hearing peers.

Ellie, noticeably uncomfortable, stood next to Brianne not knowing what her role was.

31

"What should I be doing?" She asked me in small signs.

"Are you going to observe the interpreted service, or let Brianne sit this one out and you do the signing?"

I was as confused as Ellie was. Brianne continued to sign and Ellie chose to stand next to her.

Bored out of my wits, I studied the classroom and spotted a bulletin congratulating the music teacher for the birth of her niece. I read the bulletin, saw the name of the niece and realized that the teacher's niece's mother was formerly my foster child's middle school teacher. I asked the music teacher if her sister was a teacher at my child's former middle school. She affirmed and my heart skipped.

During the lunch break in the teacher's lounge, I told Brianne that the music teacher's sister was my child's former middle school teacher… and that there were problems between us.

Monday, October 27

In the hallway, the music teacher gave me a cold stare and snubbed her nose at me. I immediately knew that she knew.

Later that day, Brianne was at her desk reading a book, and I took the opportunity to ask her about the music teacher's attitude toward me.

"The music teacher seemed friendly and happy when she heard that your child was in her sister's classroom," Brianne said.

"I guess the weekend somehow changed her mood huh?" I signed.

When Brianne asked her about it, the music teacher replied that she had no knowledge about my child and that she has always been shy, keeping to herself. Funny, she was none of those things before she found out about my problems with her sister.

That afternoon, the music teacher walked into Mrs. Jones' room and handed Mrs. Jones and each of the interpreters a piece of paper. She glanced at me and left the room with a wicked grin on her face.

Pamela walked over to me and handed me the paper. It was a coupon for a retail store. I asked her why she did not want it.

"I am 57 years old. These clothes are for the twenty-somethings. Did you get one?" Pamela answered.

I shook my head no.

"Oh! Then here, keep it," She casually replied.

Monday, November 3

Over on the East coast, I visited my friend and the Deaf school where she worked as a teacher. I wanted to see the second and third grade classrooms at the Deaf school and compare them to the second and third grade classrooms at Knight.

The second grade class at the Deaf school was taught by a culturally Deaf person. I learned that the students at the Deaf school had far better literacy and social skills than the deaf students at Knight. I asked the Deaf teacher how this was possible.

"The majority of the students' parents communicate with them in sign language, and they have a much higher involvement in their children's academic development," the teacher said.

"Involvement? Like, meaning what?" I asked.

"Whenever I ask the parents to help out in the classroom with reading and other volunteer services, the response is always greater than expected. As a result, the reading levels, social norms, conversational skills, and rules of communication are all higher," the teacher replied.

"An obvious contrast with the inclusive deaf students," I said.

I continued to observe the students at the Deaf school. It was amazing to see how they interacted! These students signed a lot quicker and incorporated abstract thoughts into their conversations. The kindergarten through fifth graders all had excellent dialogue skills, and they appropriately executed taking turns in a timely manner.

It would be helpful if the deaf students at inclusive schools had a better support system. Clearly, the listening devices and speech therapies were not doing what they were supposed to be doing.

Generally, in the public schools, the regular teachers have "roll calls" (homeroom) where they have the official head count of all students 'assigned' to their classes (usually 20-24 students). So, the deaf kids are assigned to their regular/homeroom teachers in order to satisfy and enforce the LRE mandate. But before going to their hearing classroom, the deaf kids go into the deaf classroom in order to set up and sync their hearing devices, and to walk with their assigned sign language interpreter to the hearing classroom (this creates stigma).

After the homeroom teacher finishes with the lesson, the hearing students start on their assigned work tasks, while the deaf students then return to the deaf classroom to get more help from the teacher for the deaf, and from the interpreters who also act as teacher's aides - all because they missed out entirely! The teacher for the deaf re-teaches them what was being taught in the hearing classroom. The microphone, the hearing aid devices, and the sign language interpreters apparently aren't enough. This has been going on for *years*. This does not happen in Deaf schools. Clearly, this is where they learn the best – by direct communication.

Monday, November 10

Back to work from my brief vacation, Mrs. Jones strolled alongside me towards the cafeteria to send the second graders for their lunch. We then went ahead to the teacher's lounge, where Mrs. Smith's class used to be. There was a woman, whom Mrs. Jones later introduced as Mrs. Weaver, sitting alone in the room eating her lunch. Mrs. Jones scanned the room deciding where she wanted to sit, finally choosing one of the two empty chairs at the round table where Mrs. Weaver was sitting.

Mrs. Weaver was a rude character in both personality and appearance. She had the kind of features that popped out at you. Her maroon nail polish was chipped beyond repair. I was about to find out that there was something far more disturbing about Mrs. Weaver than simply her unkempt appearance.

Mrs. Jones signed discreetly with a bite of food in her mouth, "Allen, Rachel and Zeke are integrated into her class."

Mrs. Weaver, also with food in her mouth, asked me an unintelligible question audibly. I could not read her lips because of the mushy chewed up food in her mouth (which I tried to avoid looking at).

Mrs. Jones missed my puzzled expression; otherwise, she would have either spoken up or interpreted the message. Not getting a response from me, Mrs. Weaver swallowed the gunk in her mouth and asked me again:

"How do you like it here?"

"It's great," I replied. "What grade do you teach?" I asked haltingly because of my 'deaf speech.'

"Third," she answered and immediately went back to the point that I was trying to avoid:

"Why does Emma chew that cord around her wrist?"

I looked to Mrs. Jones for permission to reveal the reason. Casually glancing back and forth between them, I explained:

"The cord is to di—."

"Libby and I are not at liberty to discuss this because..." Mrs. Jones jumped in, signing and speaking.

"What is it exactly that you do with Emma?" Mrs. Weaver interrupted, focusing her eyes on me.

"I shadow Emma," I attempted to explain further.

"Oh! You should wear a matching cord, because you are with her all the time, like her personal servant!" Mrs. Weaver laughed sarcastically, spitting food as she did.

My mouth dropped wide open and I retorted, "Excuse me, I am a college..."

I was going to say 'educated woman', but Mrs. Weaver interrupted me with more mean comments about Emma and the other deaf students.

By this time, other teachers and interpreters had filed into the room for their lunch.

Mrs. Jones attempted to reason with Mrs. Weaver, but Mrs. Weaver continued her outbursts of sadistic insults. Some of the other teachers in the room objected to her behavior, but Mrs. Weaver simply talked over them. Only one teacher and two interpreters laughed with her. The rest of us sat there silently, infuriated by Mrs. Weaver's ignorant comments.

After recess, I was teaching Emma how to hang up her coat in her locker when Carmen walked up.

"How's it going?" She'd asked me that every day since I started.

"Mrs. Weaver was mean to me. She said that Emma and I should wear matching wrist cords, because I wait on her hand and foot," I struggled to fight back the lump in my throat.

"Oh, that is only because Mrs. Weaver feels that Emma is in the wrong program," Carmen explained defensively.

Fully aware that Emma was watching our private conversation, I turned my back to her and used my body to block her line of sight.

"What program should she be in?" I signed, completely annoyed.

"Mrs. Weaver thinks she should be in the program for autistic children. The appropriate placement for her is not here." Carmen said.

"But, Emma is linguistically behind. She is frustrated because she is unable to communicate fluently. Her inability to express her ideas and feelings is the reason for her behavior. Does not this D/HH program provide excellent language support in reading and writing? Right?" I asked.

"I still think otherwise. Emma has the traits of an autistic child," she said shrugging as she walked away with her hands flailing in the air.

I steamed to myself, "What does she know!"

I didn't know it at the time, but Carmen's comment was the beginning of a change in my view of the LRE, which is defined as the educational situation in which a child with disabilities can receive what he or she needs in order to get an equal education, while being educated alongside peers who are not disabled.

About 20 minutes later, Mrs. Weaver and Interpreter Lauren came down to Mrs. Jones' class looking for me. When Mrs. Weaver's eyes met mine, she gestured for me to join her in the hallway. I went into the hallway, wondering if she had come to apologize. Out of the corner of my eye, I noticed that Mrs. Jones had trailed behind us.

As soon as I looked at Mrs. Weaver, Lauren began translating:

"You totally misunderstood me. My comments are not what you think they meant. I did not say those things. I care too greatly for these children. If you have any problems with me, you talk to me. Is that understood?!"

They left as quickly as they appeared.

I watched in disbelief as the women stormed down the hallway. Mrs. Weaver had, in fact, mocked me and the deaf students in the teacher's lounge. I immediately knew that Carmen was the person responsible for this episode.

"What happened?!" Mrs. Jones asked me in sign language.

I explained to her my earlier conversation with Carmen. Mrs. Jones threw her arms up in the air and said, "Carmen, Lauren and Mrs. Weaver are rather chummy." She finished off with first two crossed fingers into the 'R' handshape, which is a gesture for 'best friends'.

That night, I instant messaged my sister Angela and narrated to her about the incident. She gave me advice that I took to heart, "Watch your back. Do not trust others, especially in the workplace. Just watch and see. You will be surprised who your friends are."

Thursday, November 13

I had always noticed that there was something unusual about Joey, especially during recess and gym. Joey ran with an odd, robot-like gait. His head barely moved when he walked, kind of like a model balancing a thick heavy book upon it. During recess, I asked Brianne about this, but she had no idea.

I studied his movements for a while, and then I realized that he ran like this because it was the only way to prevent his cochlear implant device from slipping out of place. When it fell off, it hung like a monkey dangling from a tree limb, bouncing against the side of his head as he ran.

Moments later, the teacher blew the whistle alerting the children that recess was over. The second grade students dropped their toys and ran for the queue. I waved at the deaf students and told them to go back and pick up their jump ropes, balls and hula-hoops. Dalton kept walking toward the door where I stood. I reminded him that he had not picked up the toys from the blacktop.

Immediately, he walked up to me then roared at me and then right in Joey's face. Concerned for Joey, I sent him to the front of the queue to spare him from Dalton's wrath. We filed into the class and Dalton roared at Joey again, inches away from his face. Dalton's face was beet red and his fists were clenched as if he were ready to punch someone or something.

Pamela and I had to do something to calm him down. I knew that he would get his act together if his recess time was threatened. We told him that if he refused to pick up the playthings the next time he was asked, he would lose his recess privilege.

Mrs. Feldman, who taught the 3rd to 5th grades, had been coming down to Mrs. Jones' class during the last period to practice phonics with the deaf students by pronouncing the words on the sound-test chart. The deaf students squirmed in their chairs as Mrs. Feldman made them recite the phonics correctly. I looked at the clock and thought about the many unfinished assignments that these students could be working on, instead of wasting time with this nonsense. This was not a required part of the school's curriculum. This was simply to help Mrs. Feldman get her phonics certification, and she was using the deaf students at Knight as guinea pigs to accomplish this.

I asked Mrs. Feldman how much longer the phonics was going to last.

"Until mid-December. The students are doing well aren't they?" she smiled obliviously.

I rubbed my temples. "This cannot be happening," I thought to myself.

Mrs. Feldman worked hard to satisfy a college course in "Mastering Phonics," which was a required course to complete her endorsement to teach deaf students. The Council of Education of the Deaf does not endorse this particular university's requirement, because it is ethnocentric. However, Mrs. Feldman was granted a temporary certificate to teach deaf students.

The problem here was not that Mrs. Feldman was practicing the phonics on the deaf students, but that the phonics was taking precedence over more important subjects. The principal signs off all of the teachers' lesson plans, so he probably knew about this.

During phonics time, Dalton wasted our time with his unwanted behavior. Toby wasted our time by not listening or following directions, and by playing with the tele-loop in his hands. Emma wasted our time with extremely inappropriate behavior. A simple observation here: many of the behavior issues could have been solved if the phonics was not introduced at all.

Joey, on the other hand, was not being challenged enough in the classroom. He was smarter than most of the other students, and he typically wasted our time by endlessly interrupting the teacher for something to keep him occupied. He wandered around the classroom, not knowing what to do next, because Mrs. Jones was busy with the other students. Typically, he ended up sitting in a corner reading an unchallenging book. When he was not reading, he watched us. I glanced at Joey from the corner of my eye as he was thumping his pencil against the book that he was supposedly reading. He had read this book numerous times because it had been in the classroom since he was in kindergarten.

Friday, November 14

Dalton was now trying to be very cooperative, trying harder to listen and to follow the rules. He knew that the recess was my wildcard. Joey and Dalton did, however, continue to bicker with each other.

Earlier that morning, Joey stood behind Dalton taunting him with a piece of paper. He slid the paper in front of Dalton's face pretending that it was not right in Dalton's face. I told Joey to sit down immediately and quit provoking Dalton. Dalton's face turned red as he stared at the assignment on his desk. There was no stopping his anger. He clenched his fists as Joey antagonized him by tapping on his leg under the table. Dalton looked like he was ready to explode, so Mrs. Jones told him to move to a different seat. Joey continued bothering Dalton, this time, sliding lower and lower in his chair, until finally only his face appeared above the desk, trying to tap Dalton with his feet.

Joey and Dalton should be in separate classrooms, if only they had more D/HH support services and a better support staff to deal with their behaviors. Unfortunately, although this was the home school for most of the local deaf students, the D/HH program was too small to accommodate the needs of every individual student. But then, due to language and social deprivation, it might be a bad idea...

Right after lunch, it was time for the second graders to go out for recess. Dalton and Toby had not put their things in their lockers as they had been instructed to do. This wasted about 15 minutes of the younger students' learning time. Mrs. Jones asked me to watch the younger students while she explained the rules to the older boys for the umpteenth time.

"All personal belongings are to either stay at home or in your lockers. Only the kindergartners have show and tell."

Mrs. Jones gave the older boys assignments to do and asked me to stay in with them as part of their detention at recess because they had been fighting earlier.

I began to worry about Emma. Who was watching her? She was outside alone with all of the other students, hearing and deaf, but thankfully nothing had gone wrong.

* * *

Later, Mrs. Jones sat on the floor with the kindergarten through second graders while they did their math work. Mrs. Jones gave each student, except for Dalton, a piece of yellow paper. Mrs. Jones explained to Dalton that she was using his paper to show the children how to create one horizontal line through two vertical lines of equal space. She told him that she would give him the paper as soon as she was finished showing the students how it was done.

As soon as the students were finished creating their six equal sized squares on the yellow paper, Mrs. Jones returned Dalton's paper to him. He looked at the paper and became visibly upset. He screamed because he did not like the way that Mrs. Jones had drawn the lines on his paper.

He accused Mrs. Jones of intentionally sabotaging and ruining his piece of yellow paper.

Mrs. Jones tried to reassure Dalton. "It doesn't matter if the lines are crooked or strait as long as there are six squares on the inside of the paper. Look at the other students' papers."

Simultaneously, all of the students' heads bent down, staring at their papers.

By the time Dalton calmed down, the class had finished with the math project and moved on to another assignment. Unfortunately, I didn't see what Emma had done but she had set Dalton off again.

Suddenly Dalton kicked a heavy wooden chair, and it harrowingly landed within a foot of the group. He screamed at the top of his lungs and slammed the door as he stormed out of the classroom. The walls rattled as he hit and kicked at the classroom door from the hallway.

Stomping back into the classroom a short time later, yelling at no one in particular, Dalton screamed:

"Why did you ruin my day?!"

Dalton flipped a Lazy-boy recliner and some of the desks at an empty spot in the room. Relieved that no one had been sitting where the chairs landed, Mrs. Jones and I prepared ourselves to shield the younger students from Dalton's wrath. Fortunately, no one was hurt.

Friday, November 21

This was a special day for the students. The music teacher and the gym teacher combined their classes into one session for fun time. This event was usually the childrens' favorite social happening, and the only time that two of the second grade classes got together.

Mrs. Jones and I waited for Brianne to come down to the classroom so that we could walk the students down to the gym. After a few minutes, Mrs. Jones became incensed and said:

"You go on. I will look for Brianne because she needs to interpret the gym class, especially for Alyssa. Brianne is not here. Unbelievable!"

"I will come back and get you if the second graders need an interpreter right away," I reassured her.

"Never mind, I am going with you," Mrs. Jones said shaking her head.

Mrs. Jones came with us to the gym and began interpreting. Brianne finally showed up and said with an apology that she had been helping Mr. Lentz with his classroom project.

Mrs. Jones huffed out of the room.

Prior to the class, the gym teacher had prepared a parachute in the middle of the floor. He was explaining the rules of the game when Emma unexpectedly jumped out of her seat crying. She ran over to the music teacher sobbing loudly and pointing at the parachute. She cried, "I scared of this 'P' thing! I don't want to touch it!"

The music teacher cruelly admonished Emma, "I cannot revolve my schedule around you! It is not fair to the others if I change my schedule just for you."

My jaw dropped at her comment. Thinking of my duties regarding Emma according to the IEP, I mustered my courage and spoke on her behalf using my best deaf speech:

"I do not think she wanted you to change the schedule. I think she simply wants to sit this one out," I said, looking at Emma. She nodded in the affirmative.

The music teacher glared at me sternly and said, "Go sit down then." She then peered around my shoulder to watch the children play the parachute game where they lifted the parachute up high above their heads and the two tagged students traded empty spots by running under the chute, before it came down on them.

Taken aback by her attitude, I calmly interrupted her observations. "You'll have to speak to Emma directly because I am not one of your students."

The teacher huffed at me and rolled her eyes. Smiling acrimoniously at Emma, she said, "You may sit this one out."

Monday, December 8

The art teacher was giving a lesson on the differences between hue and tint. I noticed that several of the deaf students incorrectly signed the word 'gray.' I took this as an opportunity to show them the correct sign for 'gray,' again.

Within my peripheral vision I saw a hand waving at me. I turned to see Brianne.

"No, the right sign for 'gray' is this way... use the manual letter for 'G' sliding across the forehead above the eyebrows." She demonstrated the sign.

I ignored Brianne's obviously patronizing tone. "Are you supposed to be interpreting? The art teacher is still demonstrating the differences between hues and tints. It looks like he is demonstrating how to create an art project. Alyssa needs you to interpret for her," I said.

"But do you realize this is the way we sign around here?" She insisted.

"I know; you told me that before," I said turning my attention from her to the deaf students. They were watching our disagreement instead of the art teacher.

I went ahead and delivered a final line to the students.

"This sign that Interpreter Brianne showed me is one of many variations. The one that I showed you is the ASL color sign, which is the way the majority of Deaf Americans sign." I demonstrated the signed word for 'gray' again with my whole set of fingers from each hand bumping at each other from front to back and vice versa. They copied my demonstration.

Brianne scowled at me.

When the art class ended, Brianne told me that I should not confuse the deaf students by introducing new signs for the words.

Later, Brianne explained that the entire point of using SEE instead of ASL in the classroom was that when she signed ASL with the deaf students, they easily confused the different signs.

"I told the students, 'It does not matter which animal you pick.' I used the ASL as you showed me. Yet they interrupted me and said, 'We have gray animal?' They are inexperienced signers," she said.

Point well taken, because the signs for 'Gray' and 'Matter' are very similar. I did not realize that Brianne had tried to adopt ASL after watching me sign with the deaf students, only to have it backfire on her. I did not realize that the deaf students would easily confuse the signs, especially for words for which there are many different signs.

However, clearly recalling the incident with Lauren and Carmen, I explained to Brianne that it was very impolite for a hearing person to criticize a deaf person's use of sign language without asking why he or she chose to use a particular sign.

That afternoon, the art class and the music class were combined again to watch the school's video of the previous year's musical program. Two of the second grade classes and the music teacher were getting ready for an upcoming winter musical presentation.

Brianne and I found a place to sit on the risers, beneath the wall mounted television and VCR, as the students sat down to watch the video. The music teacher started the tape, walked briskly out of the room, and sat on the floor with the gym teacher. About five minutes later, Brianne got up and made her way to the back of the room to join the two teachers who were teasing each other intimately.

Perplexed at Interpreter Brianne's conduct, I signed with caution, as not to distract the students:

"Are you not going to interpret the video of the music program for the deaf students?"

She tilted her head up higher to maintain eye contact, raising her hands above the student's heads and signed from across the room:

"They were in this musical program last year... before you were hired. They already know the songs."

I rolled my eyes and thought, "Another of the many IEP violations going on around here."

Emma, being newly enrolled this year, was not here last year. How was she supposed to understand the video? There were some new hearing students here this year, but they could understand what was going on. This was simply unfair to Emma. Interpreters are paid to serve the needs of the deaf students, not to socialize.

After the recess, I walked the deaf second graders back to Mrs. Jones' class. The music teacher stood by the doorway with Mrs. Jones. She had a smug look on her face as I passed.

Mrs. Jones told me that the music teacher had said that I was distracting the class by talking to the interpreter. My mouth dropped.

"Is it wrong to ask the interpreter for her services, as required by the IEP?"

Neither Mrs. Jones nor Brianne understood the speed of my signs, so I gave up. Mrs. Jones insisted that we do not casually chat in the classrooms. Brianne and I looked at each other with our eyes wide open in disbelief.

I dared not point out that it was Brianne and the two special-related teachers who chatted with each other for the last 45 minutes of the video. A cliché had popped into my head: "The squeaky wheel does not necessarily get oiled; it gets replaced."

Emma had not received any interpreter service, but I did not want to cause any tension and potentially get myself fired.

Later, in the teacher's lounge, I told Cassie and Mrs. Feldman about the stunt that the music teacher had pulled. Several of the staff said that I was not alone. Cassie told me about a time when Lauren reported to the principal that Mrs. Feldman had left 15 minutes early.

"I'm confused. What do you mean by that?"

"The point is that Lauren did not even ask Mrs. Feldman why she left early. She went straight to the principal's office," Cassie signed as Mrs. Feldman looked on.

"But the principal already knew that," Mrs. Feldman elaborated. "I had already informed him that I had an appointment to meet with one of the deaf student's parents at the AEA's main office. It is just that the backstabbing environment is bad around here."

"So you are telling me that Lauren was trying to get you fired?" I asked, realizing that I was the latest victim of this cut-throat game.

Mrs. Feldman nodded her head aggressively, devouring the last of her chocolate chip cookie.

An idea popped in my head. "Why don't I try to set up a kind of service that oversees all interpreting situations and interpreters?"

Mrs. Feldman and Cassie intently watched my signing, fascinated with what I was suggesting.

"Since I am working on my BA and a certification in Deaf Studies and ASL, I could volunteer to serve as the head interpreter, overseeing the interpreters' ethics, offering refresher courses and one-on-one consultations, rotating interpreters' duties, and many more things," I signed eagerly.

Mrs. Feldman immediately blew off my idea. "That is the D/HH teachers' job. Mrs. Jones, Mrs. Smith, and I have been doing this forever." She continued shaking her head long after she'd finished her comment.

I tried to clarify my point, "I see. However, you and the other D/HH teachers are often swamped with work. The Interpreters continue to violate the code of Professional Conduct on a daily basis. A couple of the interpreters could use refresher courses in sign language."

Cassie smiled, "I know who you are talking about." Mrs. Feldman continued to dismiss my suggestion, gently shaking her head no.

After the disappointing conversation with Mrs. Feldman in the teacher's lounge, I went downstairs and brought up the idea with Mrs. Smith and Mrs. Jones. They rejected my idea as well.

I felt let down by the lack of support. Someone had to speak up for these students.

Tuesday, December 16

Mrs. Feldman got my attention when I walked into the school. She complained to me that she took an opportunity to help Amanda, a hard of hearing fifth grader, with her math. Amanda's teacher, Mrs. Clark, found out about it and fussed at Mrs. Feldman.

"You are undermining my teaching," Mrs. Clark relayed the conversation with Mrs. Feldman. "Amanda is my student, she is my responsibility."

"Yes, true, but she is also part of the D/HH program. She is integrated into the classroom with hearing students, but she also has a right to receive more help with academics because of her hearing loss. Not only that, the IEP states that she will get extra help from the D/HH teacher."

Mrs. Clark continued to reject Amanda's IEP requirements, and that is a violation of her IEP agreement.

Mrs. Feldman walked me back to Mrs. Jones' room and we spotted Amanda in the hallway crying. Mrs. Clark was speaking to her without an interpreter's assistance. This was another IEP violation.

The gym and the music teachers threw fun parties for the entire day. They provided punch, drinks, popcorn and a PG-rated movie. The deaf and hearing students sat on the gymnasium mats. The third, fourth and fifth graders attended the party in the morning. The kindergarten through second graders had their party in the afternoon. I went with the first and second graders.

There were three long rows with 25 students in each row. Timmy and Alyssa found a place to sit together in the third row against the wall. Dalton, Joey and Toby sat elsewhere with their hearing peers. Alyssa and Timmy looked around and saw me sitting with Emma in the back of the gym, near the entrance door. Timmy watched Alyssa as she walked over to me and fitfully signed, "Sign me. See movie."

47

"You want me to interpret the movie for you?" I signed with a puzzled expression.

Alyssa grinned and nodded affirmatively.

How am I, a profoundly deaf woman, going to interpret this movie? Where was the promised interpreted service? Captioning was not set up because the special related teachers did not turn on the closed-captioning mode, or the movie projection was not equipped with a closed captioning device. This was yet another IEP violation, because the deaf students did not have the same access as their hearing peers.

I looked around the darkened gymnasium for Brianne, because interpreting was her job. When I spotted her, I got up and went over to where she was to get a better look. She was sitting in the hallway next to the gym with a pile of papers on her lap. Mr. Lentz sat with his grade book in his lap. Their legs were touching.

I tapped Mr. Lentz on the foot with my own foot to get his attention. I asked them if the deaf students could have an interpreter come inside and interpret the movie. I shook my hands to signify "Come on" and pointed to the movie.

They whispered to each other. Brianne turned to look at me, signing and speaking at the same time, "No. I am busy helping Mr. Lentz with his papers. You know, calculating the percentages and scores and filling in his grade book."

Mr. Lentz turned and looked at me with a smug expression on his face, nodding his approval. Brianne's job was to interpret for the deaf students, not to be his lovelorn personal assistant.

Perturbed, I turned around and nearly bumped into several crying kindergarten students who were standing in the hallway crying because they were too afraid to be in the gym watching the monstrous dog clip in the video. The music teacher looked harried as she tried to calm the terrified children.

Just then, the principal walked by, passing Brianne, Mr. Lentz, and the music teacher. He immediately stopped in his tracks with crooked eyebrows and a bewildered smirk. He stepped back and peered inside the gym. It looked like he was going to drop the papers in his hand. He approached the music teacher, confronting her. I read his lips. He was saying that he had not been informed of the movie event.

48

Nearing the end of the day, the principal sent out an email to all of the Knight staff expressing his disapproval. He said that he felt undermined because the movie event had been held without his prior consent. He said that he did not appreciate that the two special-related teachers wasted the student's learning time. He was outraged that they would do this, considering that many of the students had speech therapies, extended hospital services, and an additional variety of private therapies during the time of the movie. These impromptu events disrupted the students' schedules, which could have been avoided had this been planned with himself and the D/HH staff.

Most of the teachers supported the special-related teachers. Personally, I figured that the deaf students go to their therapies on a weekly basis. Missing a few sessions didn't seem to hurt them. They weren't dying of deafness.

Friday, December 19

A few hours before the winter musical program, Mr. Lentz went to the music teacher's class to retrieve his students. The music teacher gave him a stack of flyers for his students to take home reminding their parents about the upcoming event.

Mrs. Jones came into the classroom and asked the deaf students where the musical program flyers were. "Parents have been calling me about date changes due to the storm," she signed to me. The students shouted out in unison, "The music teacher gave them to Mr. Lentz!" I immediately read Dalton's lips, since his were the easiest to read.

Mrs. Jones, wisely not wanting Brianne to go upstairs unsupervised, sent me with her to get the flyers from Mr. Lentz.

Brianne and Mr. Lentz argued in front of the hearing students before Brianne exasperatedly looked for the flyers herself. The students were giggling at what they saw. Annoyed, Mr. Lentz asked Brianne what she was looking for. Brianne screamed at him, "Where are the flyers for the deaf students' take home folders?!"

Mr. Lentz's face paled, "What? The deaf students need them?"

Inconvenienced by his ignorant reply, Brianne yelled, "Yes!"

"They… they're deaf! You know how they sound!" Mr. Lentz stammered searching for words.

"Where are the flyers?" Brianne asked again, obviously irritated.

Mr. Lentz pointed to the trash can.

"Ugh!" Brianne rolled her eyes. "Oh, that's right; you're new here. The deaf children can sing and play instruments!" Mr. Lentz rolled his eyes back.

The students burst out in uncontrollable laughter as Brianne's body disappeared into the four foot tall trash can, fishing out the flyers.

Mrs. Jones was very disappointed that Mr. Lentz did not give the deaf students their flyers. He was the homeroom teacher for the integration class.

"These students are on Mr. Lentz's roll call list," Mrs. Jones signed. "There is no special roll call for the deaf students in the integrated classes that the special-related teachers could have used. The D/HH teachers are constantly ignored, excluded, and overlooked by the teachers from the hearing classrooms. I hate this!"

Later that morning, Mrs. Feldman emailed me about a local news show that was going to do a feature on Allen, one of our students, and his successful CI story. When we met in the teacher's lounge, she told me that the reporter would be filming her class and interviewing Allen about the cochlear implant and his integration into the hearing classroom. The Knight staff was thrilled about the story.

I sighed for a while before responding. "When will the news be aired?"

"Tonight and every day until Christmas," Mrs. Feldman continued.

One of the hearing teachers said something to Mrs. Feldman that I didn't quite get. Mrs. Feldman replied:

"No, at first it was not a successful CI. He had a bad infection in one of his ears, so they had to do a second surgery in the other ear. After that it worked out well."

"Well, maybe the failed first attempt will be included in the program," I thought to myself. "Surely they won't be selectively biased and filter out information that they don't think viewers want to see."

As school ended, Mrs. Jones asked me if I was coming to the musical. Watching the deaf students being made a spectacle of was the last thing I wanted to do; and, I wanted to see how the news handled the Allen story.

That night, I sat with my friends on the sofa and browsed the TV to find the right station. The reporter told the story about Allen's successful CI and that now he was in the 'Normal' classroom all day with the 'Normal' students. It was truly a miraculous gift.

"Did that reporter just say that it was a miraculous gift that Allen is now enrolled in the 'normal' classroom?!" I fumed.

My friend stared at the television in disbelief. She sarcastically signed, "Define normal."

I lightly elbowed her arm. "No! The reporter's implication is that deaf classrooms for deaf students are not normal! He's saying that deaf students are not 'normal.' He could have at least chosen a word like 'hearing' over the ethnocentric word, 'normal'!"

I emailed everyone in my address book and told them that what the reporter had said was biased.

A couple weeks later, after a tumultuous debate, the reporter emailed to complain to me and Mrs. Feldman about the angry emails he'd received from the Deaf community. I replied to his email and explained that what he'd said was biased, but that I had not intended for him to receive angry emails from the Deaf community. He contended, defending his words, saying that he had researched the topic and decided that it was fair and balanced reporting.

The News was never seen in the same way again after that betrayal.

51

"But people who think they can project themselves into deafness are mistaken because you can't. And I'm not talking about imagining what a deaf person's whole life is like, I even mean just realizing what it is like for an instant."

Richard Masur

SECOND SEASON

Tuesday, January 6, 2004

During the lunch break on our first day back to school from winter break, Mrs. Jones sat next to me and struck up a casual but intriguing conversation.

"You should have seen Emma during the winter musical," she said ruefully.

"Go ahead," I said, perching my hand on my chin.

Apparently, Emma got totally lost and directionless without my presence. She fell apart and bawled in the middle of the transition from singing to walking over to the musical instruments. Emma did not know which instrument she was supposed to be playing, because she was accustomed to the familiar seating arrangement in the music class and with the familiar placement of the instruments. At the musical, the instruments were placed elsewhere, and she was up there in front of her parents as well as all of the other students' parents with the lights dimmed. All of this probably confused her.

My heart sank for Emma.

Friday, January 16

Some of the older students were putting on a skit for the younger students. Donna and I sat with the students as the performance started.

Donna asked me if she should interpret. I nodded "Yes," but she made no move to stand up. Then, trying to conceal her message from the others, Donna signed something in very small space. I didn't catch what she said, so I leaned in closer and asked her to clarify what she'd said. With bigger spatial signs, she told me to look at the back of the room.

Brianne was sitting in the back of the class with Mr. Lentz. Their thighs were touching.

While I was observing them, Donna slapped me on the arm as Brianne leaned intimately close to Mr. Lentz and whispered something in his ear that made his face turn red. He grinned. Brianne grabbed the video recorder that was sitting on Mr. Lentz's lap and took charge of recording the skit.

Timmy and Alyssa switched their gaze back and forth between Donna and Brianne. Donna ordered them to watch the skit and try to understand better by paying attention.

Yeah, right! She should have used the word, "try to 'guess' better," instead of saying, "try to 'understand' better." Hastily, I intercepted Timmy and Alyssa's attention.

Signing in ASL I asked, "What you look?" Timmy answered, pointing at the skit, "Not understand."

"Need an interpreter?" I asked.

They both nodded affirmatively. I looked at Donna and suggested that she go ahead and interpret.

"I interpreted all day and my hands are tired. These are Brianne's students," Donna replied non-sympathetically.

Careful not to step on the little fingers on the floor, I made my way to the front of the room and plopped myself down within arm's reach of Timmy and Alyssa. I don't like to sit too closely to people when I sign. It is kind of like reading a large print book one inch away from your eyes.

The skit was a familiar story, "The Little Red Hen." I could interpret that for them because I knew the story well. I turned around to look at the skit behind me and surmised where they were. Timmy and Alyssa laughed at me as I embellished the skit in ASL.

With only a few minutes left, Brianne walked over and told me to take a break. Just as I made my way back to my seat, Mrs. Jones walked in.

Donna looked at me and subtly signed, "She must have known that Mrs. Jones was coming. She's saving her own ass!"

I did not know how to react to her display of hypocrisy.

Tuesday, February 17

I trailed behind Mrs. Smith, who went into Mrs. Jones' classroom and began to cry. Mrs. Smith said that one of her students, Jaber, was about to be transferred to an oral institution in the Mid-West in less than two weeks. She was frantic because the oral institution was not the proper educational placement for Jaber.

> "Jaber had a CI implanted in one of his ears, and it failed. So, six months later, his parents had another CI performed, this time on his other ear. That one failed too." Mrs. Smith cried.

With two failed CIs, any residual hearing that Jaber had was destroyed forever. Had his parents stopped after the first failed implant, Jaber could have still used a BTE hearing aid in the functional deaf ear and been able to hear some. Now, he would never hear anything at all, ever again.

Mrs. Smith went on to say that Jaber's language acquisition in sign language and speech had been improving steadily, because he had become more receptive to his visual environment due to the constant exposure to visual language.

I asked Mrs. Smith what compelled Jaber's parents to send their deaf son to an oral school. I was shocked when Mrs. Smith said that Jaber's parents were friends with the parents of a deaf girl who had attended Knight many years ago. The interpreters and I found a place to sit down as Mrs. Smith continued.

> "Jaber's parents asked the deaf girl's parents for their opinion. Her parents decided to let their daughter explain from their own experience because she has CI and she is now an adult. It seems that she told Jaber's parents, 'Do what you feel is right'."

I wondered who the deaf woman could be. The community had committed a lot of time and effort to make sure that Jaber could stay in the Knight D/HH program. For Jaber, Knight was by far the more appropriate learning environment. It occurred to me that if Knight insisted that Jaber attend speech classes and music lessons, then perhaps, a Deaf school would be the better option. But to make a totally deaf and mute child speak defeats the purpose of oralism. (The purpose of oralism is to teach the mostly-deaf children to learn to make correct sounds aloud so their hearing parents can understand them, and to correctly interpret whatever remaining limited sounds they can still hear). The noblest thing that the oral (speech/hearing) academy could have done in this case would have been to decline Jaber's application.

After Mrs. Smith left, the interpreters and I prepared the children for the field trip to the Roundup FunVenture club house, where all the special education programs in the county met to do crafts, dance to music, and eat snacks. I felt that deaf education should not be part of the special education program because the educational approaches and disabilities were different. What sets deaf students apart from otherwise mentally delayed children is whether their development is delayed in one, multiple, or in the whole aspect/s of their abilities. Deaf children have the same capabilities as hearing children if given a visual language. As simple as it really is, Deaf people are a linguistic minority, and they just need the visual access.

The event was held at a round shaped pavilion situated next to a large river that coursed through the city. The deaf students from Knight sat in the middle of the floor with the special education students. Cassie translated. Carmen stood about 15 feet behind the group conversing with a woman and pointing at the deaf students. I read Carmen's lips in disbelief. The woman nodded her head as Carmen spilled details about the group. Brianne revealed her suspicions to me that Carmen was gossiping to a complete stranger about the group. Brianne then walked over to a crafts display near where Carmen and the woman stood. Brianne casually checked out the crafts as she eavesdropped some more.

"She is talking about your job and the deaf children's personal problems," Brianne said when she returned.

"It is none of her business to be telling a complete stranger about me and the deaf students!" I was furious.

On the bus back to school, I confronted Carmen about her agenda with a complete stranger. I reminded her that it was disrespectful to the students and their parents.

Cassie, Brianne and Donna had my back.

55

The program was clearly not closely guarded, to protect the rights of the students, and as a result, it provided a topic for gossip to those who were not involved in it.

Wednesday, February 18

It was time to go to Mr. Lentz's 2nd grade class. Mrs. Jones told the students to write at least four sentences either about personal news or about Mr. Lentz's generic Social Studies lessons. Mrs. Jones told them that I would be there to help. She warned them that if they were caught playing I was going to tell her about it.

The students lined up while I asked Mrs. Jones if she would come and observe the computer lab.

"I do not have the time. You know I don't have any prep time," she said wearily.

I thought about it for a second and said, "Why don't you ask Mrs. Smith if you can borrow Interpreter Cassie?"

"I tried. I have already asked her if I could borrow her assistant twice a week for a couple of hours, but she said that was a violation of her contract."

"But her students nap for an hour and a half, and you do not have any break at all. On top of that, her students are only at one grade level, pre-k." I paused for a moment and continued, "I mean … Mrs. Smith is being inconsiderate."

Mrs. Jones' eyes brimmed with tears. It broke my heart to see her like this, but there was no time to discuss the matter further. I had to take the students to the library and meet with Mr. Lentz's hearing students before taking the integrated group to the computer lab to do assignments.

Mr. Lentz gave a lesson about airplanes, and then we took the students to the lab. The deaf students were playing with the interfaces on the word program. Toby printed out three papers, but since he only knew a few signs, he could not explain to me why he did it.

I strolled across the room and reminded them not to break the rules and to ask permission before they printed anything. The hearing students were allowed to print, but the deaf students were not because they had goofed around the other day, not completing the assignments. They were disregarding the assignment that Mrs. Jones had given them. It became challenging after a while.

Walking back and forth across the room to help not only the deaf, but the hearing students too, tired me out. There was something about the seating assignments that nagged me. I analyzed the seating placements and it dawned on me that the deaf students were spread out across the room and the hearing students were not. It would make more sense to keep the deaf students together so that I and the interpreters could better observe and communicate with them. I turned to look for Mr. Lentz, but he was nowhere to be seen.

After the lab, I took the deaf students back to Mrs. Jones' room and reported their behaviors to her. Mrs. Jones was visibly upset and asked:

"Where is Brianne?"

"I think you will have to ask her yourself," I replied.

Brianne showed up a few minutes later and announced that she had been upstairs, helping Mr. Lentz finish his airplane model. She was now where she was supposed to be in the first place.

"Wow! You should see their airplane models," she giggled awkwardly.

Brianne was obviously smitten with Mr. Lentz, a bachelor. Unfortunately, I had learned, she was married to someone else…

Later, during my lunch break, I waited in the teacher's lounge for Mr. Lentz to show up. He never did. I wanted to share my idea with him, so I went upstairs and found him in his classroom. I walked in without knocking. He seemed to be annoyed at my presence. Brianne was sitting rather close to him behind his desk.

Using sign and not voice, I said to Brianne, "I need to speak with him alone."

Brianne appeared to be surprised, "Is everything OK?" she signed back.

I was frustrated and signed a bit too harshly, "It has nothing to do with you."

57

Brianne left the room and I plopped down where she'd been sitting. "Hi. I wanted to talk to you about something."

Mr. Lentz nodded but then turned his back to me and began surfing the web. "Well, I'm waiting…" He turned toward me just long enough to say it, then he instantly turned back toward the computer.

"Please turn and face me while I am talking," I said patiently. It shouldn't have to be pointed out that even lip-reading is a visual language.

Mr. Lentz swiveled around, slumped in his leather chair and stared at me.

"OK. I would like for all the deaf students to sit on the same row in the lab so that it will be easier to supervise their work progress. It is difficult to look after their work if they are seated separately around the lab with more than 30 desks and computer monitors blocking their faces."

"I placed them in those positions for a reason; if they sit together, they talk and bother each other." Mr. Lentz said making a peculiar face.

"There are hearing children in there that need to be separated too! Why target only the deaf students? I need your help by staying in there with your class. Either that, or keep Brianne with the deaf students," I shot back angrily.

Mr. Lentz tilted his head slightly backwards, tapping his index finger on his lips thoughtfully. He seemed taken aback. At least I spoke my piece.

Monday, February 24

It was a bright gleaming morning and I was preparing to begin the day. I noticed that there was an extra take home box mixed in with the others. The name tag said "Eli," and had his school picture on it. I turned to Mrs. Jones and pointed to the box. She said that Eli was a new student in the class who would be starting that day.

I walked out into the hallway and saw three of the interpreters - Lauren, Donna, and Cassie - waiting for the buses to unload.

"Did you know that Eli was transferred to Mrs. Jones' room?"

They nodded in affirmation. I asked them about Eli's situation. They were not sure what I meant, so I clarified that Eli was transferred into the class and no one ever told me about having a new student.

"I am not surprised," Lauren said.

"Oh, I knew about Eli," Donna chimed in as if it made no difference that I was left out of the loop.

"You know, I was the preschool interpreter in Mrs. Smith's class when Eli was in there. His lips were always red and swollen from constantly licking them," Cassie said.

Cassie then began telling us that Mrs. Smith used to pick up the students by their overall straps. She said that Mrs. Smith particularly picked on Eli. Mrs. Smith would scream at him, "Put your nasty tongue back in your mouth!" As a result of Mrs. Smith constantly screaming at him, Eli cried a lot and licked his lips incessantly.

Apparently everyone knew about the situation between Mrs. Smith and Eli.

Monday, March 1

Mrs. Jones had been looking forward to a new schedule that provided her 45 minutes of prep time without the first graders in class. Having Eli in the class, a pre-k student, changed that. Eli's parents and Mrs. Smith were at odds with each other, so he was transferred to Mrs. Jones' classroom in order to pacify the parents.

Mrs. Jones personally told the principal that she felt like Eli's baby sitter and that she believed her classroom was unsuited for him. Having him in the class greatly diminished the time she could spend with the other students. She got through the day by finding things for him to do, but she simply did not have age appropriate materials for him.

The principal said that he understood, and he reassured her that no one was complaining and that the parents were happy with the arrangement.

Keeping Eli entertained was overwhelming. Mrs. Jones had to stay in the classroom with Eli while the first and second graders were with the special-related classes. Deaf students from each grade level had their own interpreter — except for Eli.

Mrs. Jones decided that she must do something about this. She told Brianne that she could no longer go upstairs and help Mr. Lentz (which in reality, Brianne was supposed to be helping the deaf students with their language acquisition anyway). Eli, who was catapulted into our classroom, was not mature enough to keep up with the rest of the students in the class, and he could benefit from Brianne's assistance. It was about time…

Tuesday, March 2

Brianne was visibly upset with Mrs. Jones. She was sullen and quiet, so I tried to allay the situation. I struck up a few funny snippets. She warmed up a bit.

"Yeah, we need help with Eli in here. He is a real handful," I casually threw in. "Mrs. Smith has an abundance of prep time while Mrs. Jones has no prep time as it is. Now she has Eli on top of everything else, and she doesn't even have an assistant for him. The principal just kind of threw him at her without discussing it with her first."

"Well, I lack the leadership and skills to guide their learning process. What's more, Mrs. Jones has no backbone. She is soft hearted and people take advantage of her."

I somewhat agreed with her. If the principal had a problem with Mrs. Smith, he should have taken care of the problem instead of making a quick fix. Mrs. Smith was, however, well protected by being a member of a large teacher's union.

In many ways, it was wonderful having Eli in our classroom, because he changed the energy and was a buffer to some of the older children's outbursts. However, it was not an ideal learning environment for him, because he had no peers his age. Trying to figure out what to do with him was touch-and-go on a daily basis. Mrs. Jones asked Mrs. Smith if she could borrow from her academic materials for students his age and return them at the end of the day. Mrs. Smith flatly said no.

Mrs. Jones' eyes filled up with tears.

After school, I spotted Eli's mother, Leah, and trotted over to get her attention before she drove off. I casually started a conversation with her about Eli. Leah expressed her gratitude for us to take him at the last minute. I thought she was going to cry as she went on about how Mrs. Smith pulled Eli's arm, lifted him by one hand, grabbed him by the shirt, or shoved him away. Eli would become very upset whenever Mrs. Smith would yell at him to shut up and tell him, "That's stupid."

Leah went on about how happy, outgoing and bubbly Eli had become since he had been in Mrs. Jones' room. This was a familiar story when it came to Mrs. Smith. Several of the interpreters had expressed concerns about her abusive conduct. Jayme, one of the interpreters who had been in Mrs. Smith's room, said that she quit when she saw the questionable psychological game unfolding in Mrs. Smith's classroom. As she left, she told me and Cassie that one of the parents wanted her to document the daily educational atmosphere that her child was subjected to:

"It started around 1999. The parents began suspecting that something was not right. Over a period of weeks, her normally outgoing son had become clingy...different. Shortly after that, the child was diagnosed with an acute separation anxiety. The parents requested permission to video tape the child's classroom for one week to rule out anything that may have caused his fearful state. The principal hesitated due to Mrs. Smith's extreme objection. She said that some of the deaf students did not turn in permission slips to be videotaped. Once that issue was resolved, the principal approved the videotaping.

The cameras were placed in the corner of the classroom, out of the children's reach. As soon as the class ended each day, the parents retrieved the tape and reviewed it at home each night.

At the end of the week, the parents requested a conference with the principal, Mrs. Smith and Jayme. The parents demanded to know why Mrs. Smith had Jayme turn the camera off and on throughout the day.

Mrs. Smith said that the children had two recess times, gym, art, music, nap and lunchtime. She said that it made no sense to leave the tape running in an empty darkened classroom. That sounded plausible, but the parents wanted to know why the tape did not show the children getting ready or lining up…"

At that point, Jayme had stood up and said, "I am quitting this job. I am a BA graduate of Social Work. The entire school's attitude stinks! However, on the grounds of abuse, Mrs. Smith comes close, but it is not enough to have her removed from the school."

Upon hearing her story, several of the interpreters and I were left speechless. What could we do?

I motioned for Jayme to meet me in the hallway. I asked her if she would like to come to the local Deaf Club with me.

Her mouth dropped open and she hugged me. "I have always wanted to visit the Deaf Club, but Carmen said that the club's secrecy is heavily guarded, and it was a sacred ritual, exclusively for deaf people. She said that a formal invitation is required."

Carmen's ludicrous comments no longer shocked me.

Wednesday, March 10

The melted snow ushered in the season of spring. It took three of Mrs. Jones' interpreters to crack open the antiquated, lofty windows. I asked around what the fuss was all about. Though the snow had melted, it was still quite cool outside. Mrs. Jones and the interpreters excitedly told me how wonderful it was to be next to the three huge crabapple trees that sprouted fragrant pink petals just outside the window. Pamela smiled and Brianne exclaimed that with the interpreter's desk next to the opened window, the fragrance of the tree's flowered petals flowed into the room as the air breezed by.

"Wow! Very pink poufy trees!" I gestured to Brianne.

"We have the best 'window office' in the entire school!"
She excitedly signed back.

For the first time since I'd been at Knight, I felt my heart warming. Maybe there was hope here, after all!

Before going to the computer lab, Mrs. Jones specifically told the students to not play with the fonts. Mrs. Jones, Brianne, the deaf second graders and I agreed that their assignments had to be completely finished before lab was over or they would have to stay inside and use their recess time to finish their assignment.

I walked the students to the lab and they logged into their computers. I worked one-on-one with Emma until she was able to work independently.

I put forth my best effort to get them moving at a quick enough pace to finish. I did not want them to miss their recess. I wanted to be outside too, rather than to stay inside with them while they finished their assignments. They have so much energy to burn, and they become restless after long periods of inactivity.

Dalton peered over Joey's monitor, pointing and talking about what was on the screen. Alyssa wandered all over the lab talking with her classmates and showing them which websites to visit. Toby did a little spelling, but he too goofed around a lot. He tended to watch out for the adults to see if they were observing his progress. When an adult would venture by to check his work, he quickly clicked the red 'X' to close the window he had open. Brianne was at the computer terminal behind Toby, surfing the internet and not paying attention to what he was doing.

Unexpectedly, Mrs. Jones briskly walked into the lab and looked directly at me. My heart skipped a beat. My eyes darted toward Brianne, who instantly popped out of her seat and trotted over to Dalton's side, pretending to look busy.

Mrs. Jones walked over to my area and checked on Emma's assignment.

Brianne stood behind Mrs. Jones and craned over her shoulder so that I could see her. With her lips pursed shut, she subtly signed, "That bitch is spying on me!" She rolled her eyes and turned back to work with Dalton. I shrugged and resumed my work with Emma.

The principal expected the interpreters to help the deaf students catch up with their work, to help them to catch up with the hearing students, and to assist the D/HH teachers by assuming the role of teacher's aide when necessary.

* * *

Later that day, Mr. Lentz gave the students a test about airplanes. The deaf students had not studied for the test, and when Brianne graded them, it showed. The deaf students had failed miserably. They often skipped doing their homework assignments. Brianne gave the grades to Mrs. Jones.

Mrs. Jones knew that something was amiss because she had personally helped them understand the lesson on airplanes herself. She reviewed the material and even checked out books from the library for them.

Mr. Lentz had only given the students about 20 minutes to do the test. The rest of the lab time had been used for reviewing for the test.

Mrs. Jones told Mr. Lentz that the deaf students needed a longer response time for each question, as stated in the IEP.

"Their IEP doesn't state untimed tests," Mr. Lentz objected.

"Yes, the IEP clearly states a longer response time per question," Mrs. Jones replied.

Upon closer inspection, Mrs. Jones noticed that Mr. Lentz had marked the answers wrong if they misspelled the words, but the students were only copying Mr. Lentz's sloppy penmanship. Mrs. Jones showed Mr. Lentz that he made the letter 'r' look like a 'v' in the word "Orville." This was a classic case of "Monkey see, Monkey do."

Mrs. Jones suggested that he should type the test over again, clarify and rephrase the questions.

The teachers sat together and gave the deaf students oral and typewritten questions about airplanes. The students spoke their answers from memory. To Mr. Lentz's amazement, the scores improved dramatically. He realized that the deaf students tended to copy whatever was shown to them, regardless of whether they understood the words or not. He learned to type the tests and to include options such as multiple choice, matching and true / false questions, rather than short essays and definitions. This helped the deaf students tremendously because their literacy skills were lower than average.

Mrs. Jones emphasized to me, "The hearing teachers here do not understand how the deaf students' minds work."

She was right. Often a deaf student's sole support on the linguistic level is at the school, from the first period to the last. This is especially true of socialization through language. Yet, there are some parents that speak four different foreign languages and refuse to learn their deaf child's native sign language.

Monday, March 22

The week following spring break, Brianne and Mr. Lentz continued their interoffice romance by touching each other inappropriately in the presence of the students. They gave each other backrubs, locked elbows, stood closely and made other public displays of affection. Brianne took advantage of the situation when Mrs. Jones was sick, which enabled her to spend most of her time in Mr. Lentz's room. Brianne did not interpret in the computer lab, so I ended up doing two jobs: hers and mine.

Mrs. Miller, the charismatic substitute teacher, visited the lab and asked me where Brianne was. I told her that she was upstairs grading Mr. Lentz's papers.

"This is not an appropriate code of work ethics. She is paid to interpret, not to grade papers. I am telling you, the principal at this school does not have the balls to fire or replace employees here," she said.

Mrs. Miller went upstairs and walked in on Brianne and Mr. Lentz with their hands interlaced. She ordered Brianne to go back downstairs and to help me manage the classroom.

Brianne bitterly stormed into the lab and started snapping at the students. I became concerned. Mrs. Miller trailed behind her and discreetly signed to me, "Report either to me or to the principal if you have any problems with her work ethic."

I nodded, trying not to give myself away.

After Mrs. Miller left, I asked Brianne if she was OK. She did not respond.

Mr. Lentz came down to the lab about five minutes before the class ended. To my horror, he slapped Brianne on the butt with the papers in his hand. I quickly scanned the room to see if any of the students had witnessed the inappropriate slap. It did not appear that they had.

The two of them strolled together toward the back of the room behind the students. They interlocked their fingers again and tucked them between their sides. Mr. Lentz was lecturing from the notes in his free hand. Brianne was all over him, not interpreting. Score that one for another IEP violation.

That afternoon before recess, Brianne stormed into the room and slammed a microphone on a poster Mrs. Miller had been preparing for a classroom discussion. After recess, Brianne stormed in the room again, yelling at the students without using sign, "Toby, Timmy and Dalton! You did not hang up your jackets or put your trainers on! Do it right now!" As soon as she stopped yelling, she disappeared into the hallway.

Mrs. Jones returned to work shortly after the second recess. Mrs. Miller relayed what had transpired while she was gone. Mrs. Jones became visibly upset with Brianne because her time with Mr. Lentz interfered with her doing her job. Mrs. Jones forbade Brianne from going upstairs while Mrs. Miller subbed.

It was about time, but it still was not enough.

Just before the last period ended, Brianne blew up to me, saying that Mrs. Jones was too weak to stand her ground against Eli's former teacher, the parents, and the school administrators who allowed such situations to continue. In this case, it was a toss-up as Brianne appeared to really care for the deaf students because she was right, but at the same time, it appeared she projected her own negligence onto others to deflect attention from herself.

Wednesday, March 31

Arriving at work, I quickly read my emails before the students came into the classroom. Both Mrs. Jones and Brianne were absent. As usual, Mrs. Miller was the substitute teacher. Pamela, Donna and I knew that Brianne was not sick. She just could not stand being in the same room with Mrs. Miller.

Cathleen, a slender old woman who was already showing signs of osteoporosis, would be substituting for Brianne that day. Every time Cathleen stood up, she hunched over, and gently swayed from side to side. Her hair was a wispy white cotton ball. Cathleen's daughter was deaf, which was used to *justify* her interpreting expertise.

Toby entered the room wearing two new ear molds, swirled blue in color. I knew that they would not last. He'd broken other ones to avoid having to wear the tele-loop device. He was the only kid in the building that had to wear the tele-loop, and he often left it lying around to avoid it like the plague.

Joey and Toby always made pained expressions when an adult handed them the microphones to pass on to the teachers. They were truly embarrassed by the stigma attached to the microphones. They knew that it set them apart from the hearing children.

Cathleen had a hard time managing Dalton and Joey. They fought all morning. Dalton was obsessed with always sitting in the exact same spot, right in the middle of the table, across from the teacher. Otherwise, he would blow up. Joey knew this and purposely pushed Dalton's buttons.

I caught Joey tapping his foot on Dalton's chair under the table. I separated the boys immediately and sat between them. Dalton blew up anyway.

Mrs. Miller and Pamela made Dalton sit in the hallway to calm down before they left to report the incident to the school counselor. Dalton banged his head and kicked the door repeatedly. Pamela returned and tried to calm Dalton down.

Mike and Timmy took this opportunity to talk about Dalton rather than to do the reading assignment that Pamela had told them to do.

"Dalton crazy again," Mike signed to Timmy.

"I know," Timmy giggled and got up from his seat acting freakishly, emulating Dalton.

The two boys carried on an enriched dialogue, a skill that did not exist in the majority of the deaf students at Knight School. Taking turns with dialogue is one of the social skills that deaf students often lacked. Those two were able to carry on clear conversations non-stop, especially without breaking eye contact, and without ever stopping others for clarification or having to ask them to repeat things.

I warned the boys to do their work and quit talking about Dalton, but when they continued, I did not enforce it.

The students were supposed to be writing about the field trip in their journals. Some of them drew pictures, some of them wrote about other things, and some even made paper airplanes. None of them did the assignment.

We tried to get Eli, who always had boundless energy, busy with things like motor coordination toys. There was very little we could do for him educationally while trying to manage kindergarten, first grade and second grade students as well.

The principal walked down the hallway toward Dalton. Dalton saw him and tried to bolt. Mrs. Miller grabbed a chair and handed it to the principal. The principal sat in the chair and held onto Dalton tightly. Dalton flailed his legs and arms and screamed. When he realized that he was trapped, he screamed louder until his face reddened.

It was difficult to get the second graders to ignore Dalton and to line up and keep moving, as I escorted them to the art class in the basement.

During the art class, I watched Cathleen interpret for the deaf students. Cathleen broke away and commented to me, "I interpret for them, and the hearing students watch me more than they do!"

While Cathleen was talking to me, Emma got frustrated, jumped up from her chair and clumsily ran across the classroom, chomping a pink eraser in half as she went. She yelled and flailed her arms spastically, and then she collapsed in the middle of the hard linoleum floor, where we allowed her to remain.

Emma slept instantly, like a kitten encountering a beam of sunlight.

The hearing students giggled uncontrollably at her antics.

Cathleen only used about 10 signs when she interpreted. She never interpreted the entire context of the lesson — only a word here and there. I wanted the principal to be able to see this for himself. Having a deaf daughter does not in itself qualify someone to be an interpreter.

At recess I stayed in to supervise Emma, who was still napping. Cathleen came in and said that the three deaf boys had been sent to the principal's office for fighting.

Reading the absentee list, I noticed that Mr. Lentz was absent that day too. My imagination ran amok.

Dalton and Joey were still fighting after recess. I threatened to take away their recess for the next day if they did not stop, and that seemed to be working. Dalton profusely apologized to Joey and Joey made the motion of apologizing back. I sent them to pack their backpacks one at a time to give them a chance to calm down.

Later that afternoon, Mrs. Miller was past schedule getting back to the classroom. It was 3:25 and Mrs. Miller had been due at 3:10. When she arrived, she said that she'd been having problems with Michelle. She said that Michelle refused to come back in and began throwing rubber playground chips at her. She tried to physically bring the child in, but Michelle bit her. Mrs. Miller had then dragged the little pint, kicking and screaming, to the principal's office.

Mrs. Jones must have forgotten to let Michelle know that Mrs. Miller would be getting her from the playground instead of Mrs. Jones.

Some things only work if trust has been earned, especially with this child.

Thursday, April 1

It was assessment week for the progress report cards. Joey's parents wanted to place him in a regular school in his home district and use an interpreter. All of the IEP team tried to convince the parents to not put Joey into his home district school. Instead, the D/HH school would withdraw Joey's interpreter at Knight and see how he adjusted.

Meanwhile, Emma was napping, so Mrs. Jones took Eli outside to assess him. Mrs. Jones placed a four-by-four inch placard on the table for Eli to look at. On the card was the picture of a kite. Beneath the kite were four letters: 'M', 'J', 'K', and 'Z'.

Eli looked at the card with intense focus, licked his lips and made the sign for 'kite' and said 'K'.

The next card showed the picture of a lion. Eli stared at the card intensely and formed a handshape resembling the manual letter, 'C' moving his hand from his forehead to the back of his neck – the signed word of 'Lion'. He moved his tongue under his top teeth and made an 'L' sound, then looked at his handshape. He looked at the teacher and said, "C" for lion. Eli relied heavily on sign language, but also had fluent speech.

The school's program was oral centered using intensive speech therapy that had no benefits academically. This was a perfect example; if the speech therapy was successful, then why did Eli not know the difference between 'C' and 'L' for the pictograph of a lion?!

Eli's parents had transferred him into Mrs. Jones' classroom and that was the end of it.

Meanwhile, Dalton was doing somersaults in the middle of the floor while waiting for his assessment. The deaf students egged him on with every somersault, giggling and squealing in their seats.

* * *

Later, Brianne and I took the deaf students to the music class. They gave their microphones to the music teacher, and as usual, she put them on the table and walked away.

She was teaching a new lesson that used traditional Polynesian instruments called 'Lummi sticks'.

The students were separated into partners and each given a foot-long stick for each hand. They were supposed to bang the sticks together, tap them on the floor, and then hit their partner's stick, in a rhythmic manner.

The deaf students had not put themselves in the best seating to see the interpreter. All but Toby had their backs to the interpreter. Toby faced the interpreter and Joey teamed up with him. Toby was not the most reliable student for the rest of the deaf students to copy. He banged his Lummi sticks in an incorrect pattern and Joey followed beat. I told Joey to watch the interpreter, but he chose to ignore my suggestion. They continued using the sticks the wrong way, sitting far from the teacher and the interpreter. None of the deaf students watched her as she sat in her chair and signed.

I suggested to the music teacher that the deaf students face her and the interpreter, but she broke her eye contact with me.

I turned to Brianne and told her how I felt about the deaf students' seating arrangement and asked her to help them to have maximum view.

"Well, they are old enough, so it is their own responsibility to make sure they are in the best position," she replied. Mrs. Jones had spent more than 10 minutes explaining to the deaf students why they should face the interpreter at all times.

She had closed with this mantra, "It's your responsibility to listen."

Eight years old is old enough? The deaf students are culturally deprived. They don't know how to utilize maximum information. They are constantly trying to act like the hearing students. They don't want to be different or embarrassed. If they sit wherever they want, to see the interpreter the best, or not, so be it, and their peers are welcomed to sit close by.

I remember going to a mainstreamed school for the first three years of my education. I was never sent to music class. What is the purpose of sending a deaf kid to music class anyway? This was definitely a new concept to me. When I asked the D/HH teachers, they said that the deaf students went to their special classes so that the regular teachers could have prep time for their lessons. Oh, that explains it...

There had also been a conundrum with Joey about where he should take his tests. I felt that he was better off in Mrs. Weaver's classroom where he went for the integration program. There were fewer distractions for him there. Academically, he performed better than the rest of the deaf students, but being among his deaf peers gave him a chance to socialize with them, and socialization was the distracting aspect for Joey. Through my personal observations, Joey rarely socialized with his hearing classmates. He looked uncomfortable when he tried. Yet, he would not be seen anywhere near his deaf peers during recess. Had he socialized more at recess, he would not have felt as compelled to talk in the classroom, since he could express himself elsewhere. The opportunity was not there for him. He typically preferred talking and socializing with his deaf peers, especially with Toby and the older deaf students, but only in Mrs. Feldman's classroom.

There was another, more unconventional, option that could have been employed while testing the deaf students: they could have removed their hearing aids and CIs. This would have removed the distracting noises and helped them to focus better. The school would have never approved such a method though — the deaf students were required to wear their mechanical ears at all times, even when it did not benefit some of them.

Monday, April 5

The deaf students tended to watch the hearing students to see what they were doing. They followed whatever the hearing students were doing. They only gave the interpreters an occasional glance, to keep up with what was going on. This frustrated Brianne, who said that she felt like a schizophrenic — talking to no one. Interpreting hurt her hands and made them go numb. It seemed pointless to her if the students were not going to pay attention. She admitted that this was one of the reasons she preferred to help the teachers grade their papers instead of interpreting for the students.

This reminded me about a story that the music teacher once told me:

"I told the class, 'Anyone with a first name that starts with a 'G' may come to the front'. Several hearing students went to the front. The deaf students followed them up. None of the deaf students' names began with the letter 'G'. During this time, both of the second grade classes were in the same music session.

"Another time, I told them, 'Mrs. Rickham's class, please stand up.' The deaf students in Mr. Lentz's class saw the hearing students in Mrs. Rickham's class stand up, so they stood up too. They had not noticed that the hearing students in Mr. Lentz's class remained seated. The naiveté of the deaf students upset the hearing students and they did not want to associate with them."

Later, in the teacher's lounge, I was talking with a few of the staff about the deaf students' not paying attention to instructions. One of the interpreters jumped in and told a similar story to that of the music teacher's.

"Libby, just before you came to work in September, the gym teacher said, 'If I shoot this ball into the hoop, Mrs. Rickham's class will start the game'. Then, the gym teacher shot the ball in the hoop successfully. Mrs. Rickham's class cheered. All the deaf students in Mr. Lentz's class cheered too.

"Several of the hearing students in Mr. Lentz's class admonished the deaf students to quit cheering for Mrs. Rickham's class. The deaf students were cheering for the opposite team and the hearing students were angry about it. No one was willing to play with the deaf students for the rest of the gym session — probably to teach them a lesson — all because of miscommunication."

One of the teachers chimed in, "No kidding? I thought that was funny!"

It is not the deaf students' fault that the information was not made available to them.

Tuesday, April 13

Both of the second grade classes went on a field trip to a nature trail center. When we arrived, we split the students into two groups; one group was the boys and one was the girls. Only one interpreter was available, and Mrs. Rickham and Brianne thought it was better if Brianne went with the girls. Brianne said that Alyssa and Emma needed an interpreter more than the boys did.

"Besides, the deaf girls can use a break from the boys," she said.

Mr. Lentz and I went with the all-boys group. During the hike, the three deaf boys grappled with what the field guide was saying. From time to time, they asked me to explain.

I made up whatever sounded right, depending on where the tour guide was standing at the time. On many occasions, out of boredom, the boys chased each other. Mr. Lentz ignored them. I felt that he should have kept more of a watchful eye on them, but again, no interpreter was present. As simple as it was, the lack of interpreter service was probably why he excused the boys' behavior.

After the hike, the two groups met up for lunch. Some of the hearing girls tried to strike up a conversation with Alyssa, who could not read lips. They finally gave up on her and moved away. I strolled over to Alyssa and sat down with her. I quizzed her in slow sign to see if she understood what the girls had said. She nodded yes.

Unconvinced, I asked what they had said. Alyssa continued to smile and nod, as she had done the entire time. "Fine," she said and took a big chomp out of her sandwich.

Mrs. Jones and Eli were sitting on the floor playing an educational game when we arrived back at the classroom. Immediately, she told Eli to clean up the game. I could tell that she enjoyed the one-on-one time with Eli.

Brianne told the second graders to come back into the classroom. The table where the deaf students usually sat was piled high with papers. There was no room for the students to sit and do their assignments. Mrs. Jones tapped my leg and asked me to clear the table. I asked her about the papers as I carefully jiggled them into one neat pile.

"These are my lesson papers. I still need time to prepare for this week's lessons. I am so behind. I never know what I will be teaching them each day."

She had been playing lesson plans by ear ever since Eli had started in her class.

When the students went out for their bathroom break, I looked at Mrs. Jones who let out a long sigh.

"I feel like I am only managing the class, like I am simply getting by from day to day, instead of teaching," she signed.

Mrs. Jones was teaching pre-k, kindergarten, first and second grade. One of the second graders had an above average intelligence, but the others fell between a kindergarten and first grade level.

Mrs. Jones and Mrs. Feldman planned to split up the current second graders in the fall. Altogether, Mrs. Feldman would have nine students: Alyssa, Dalton, Allen, Rachel, Zeke, Stewart and Thomas, and two new students, a third grader named Brendan and a fifth grader named Josiah. All three older boys — Allen, Zeke, and Stewart — had CIs.

Mrs. Jones would have a total of seven students: Timmy, Emma, Joey, Toby, Eli, a girl from Mrs. Smith's class named Isabella, and a newcomer named Paxton — all of them on three different grade levels.

"Wow! Mrs. Smith has only four deaf students next fall," I commented.

"Yes and four hearing students. Mrs. Smith felt the deaf students could use role models," Mrs. Jones replied.

"Role models? What are the deaf children doing wrong that it warrants hearing students to role model for them?" I was stunned.

"No, it's more like integration preparedness, like citizenship education," she clarified.

"Are you saying that deaf children are so ill prepared that they need a hearing role model to help them learn to behave like a hearing person?"

"No. It's more like socialization. The deaf students need a lot of work on their communication skills. That's all I know, based on what Mrs. Smith told me."

Unbelievable. Common ground does not exist when neither the hearing nor the deaf students share accessible communication, as is true for most pre-kindergarteners.

The hearing students would develop communication skills in all their classes. However, the D/HH classroom is often the only place and the only opportunity that D/HH students can see and interact with their deaf peers. Now they would be separated and marginalized *again* by being segregated within their own inclusive/deaf classroom!

Mainstreaming hearing students into the deaf program would only hinder the deaf students' social growth. It is difficult for deaf students to socialize with hearing students. The hearing students, talking at a normal rate for hearing people to understand them, are actually moving their lips at warp speed for their deaf classmates. They turn their backs, move their heads, break eye contact, cover their mouths with their hands, and commit a variety of other common behaviors that work well enough when communicating with people who can hear them, but they are not conducive to communicating with someone who is trying to read their lips.

Putting hearing students into the deaf classroom would only interfere with the deaf students' social development. It would only split up the deaf students culturally. If a deaf-mute child is in the same kindergarten class with an orally proficient kid who is deaf, and they are both only beginning to learn signed words, the deaf-mute child will be left out. The hearing students will seek out the orally proficient deaf students' friendship and leave out the deaf-mute student.

This ended up being the case with two deaf pre-kindergarteners, Blossom and Sidda, in Mrs. Smith's class. Sidda spoke well and was able to socialize with the hearing students. Blossom did not. The hearing pre-k students flocked to Sidda because she spoke well, while Blossom was left out.

If Blossom and Sidda had both been in Deaf school, it would have been Sidda who got left out because of her tendency of using her preferred method of communication – voice. Sidda's tendency of using her voice would probably diminish once she picked up sign language but again, there's no chance she would end up at the Deaf school as Knight school was an ideal environment for her which means Blossom's education was severely compromised. But while bad habits can be unlearned, initial learning requires an input-nourishing environment, in order for the correct details to be efficiently absorbed the first time.

Since not all D/HH students are able to learn to speak fluently, it is best to teach them sign language early. There is no way of knowing which deaf student will need to acquire sign language skills. The deaf support service is designed to help the students acquire language, not to make them hearing-like.

This integration approach was very unequal for them.

Friday, April 16

Friday was a special day. Both of the second grade classes met at the soccer field with the gym and music teachers. It was Mr. Lentz's class versus Mrs. Rickman's class.

Brianne pulled all of her deaf students together and asked them if they understood the rules. They all nodded yes and ran back to the soccer field.

When the game began, Mr. Lentz's class was on the north side of the soccer field. Mrs. Rickman's class was on the south side. For some unexplained reason, Joey kept kicking the ball into his own goal. As he did that, Mrs. Rickham's class cheered and Mr. Lentz's class angrily yelled at him to stop. Brianne walked over and warned him not to do it anymore, but Joey continued to kick the ball into his own goal. Brianne finally told him that if he did it again, he would sit out for the rest of the game.

It was so disheartening to see Mrs. Rickham's class try and take advantage of the situation. It was not Joey's fault. Joey's hearing loss did not cause him to do this. The Deaf students at their Deaf schools do not typically do what he just did.

"Did the teacher say that he would sit out for the rest of the game if he kept on doing that?" I asked Brianne.

Shaking her head no, she explained, "The special-related teachers and the teachers of the hearing students do not care about the deaf students. They always let the interpreters take charge of the deaf students. I feel compelled to intervene or they will look stupid."

Brianne and I continued looking at each other, wondering if Joey understood the rules of the game.

Moments later, Brianne changed her mind and took him out of the game anyway. She explained the rules to him again and asked him if he understood. Joey nodded eagerly, staring past her at the field.

I glanced over at Alyssa. She was repeatedly kicking the ball out of bounds. I told Brianne to watch Alyssa, who excitedly kicked the ball out of bounds again. Brianne walked over and told the special-related teachers. They giggled, forgetting that they were wearing the microphones around their necks.

To spare Alyssa any further humiliation, I walked over and asked her why she kept kicking the ball out of bounds.

"Hold ball throw back play," she signed.

Her inconsistent reply set me back. In the simplest terms I could find, I explained that it was not to her team's advantage for her to continue kicking the ball out of bounds.

"I hold throw," she signed.

"You like to hold the ball and throw it back to your team?" I asked.

She nodded enthusiastically and ran off to play some more of the game in her own unique way.

The hearing students were following the rules and the deaf students were not. The deaf students were unintentionally embarrassing themselves, yet none of the available adults stepped in to demonstrate how the game was played. If they had been at Deaf school, they would not have embarrassed themselves like this, because there would be communication going on between peers.

Monday, May 3

Mrs. Jones told the deaf students that there were new rules on printing in the lab. Joey verbally interrupted Mrs. Jones and told her that he did not want the font set at 12. Mrs. Jones reminded him to raise his hand before speaking. Mrs. Jones and the deaf students compromised and selected a font and type-face. She wanted me to set the defaults, which I did.

"That's final! Leave the defaults alone," I declared.

The deaf students agreed.

Brianne and I also told Dalton not to interfere with Joey's assignments. Dalton fervently worked on his assignments while Joey bothered him. Dalton typically needed extra help, while Joey was usually way ahead of the rest of the class. This was when Joey would get restless and goof around.

Brianne and I ordered Joey to do his own work and leave Dalton alone. Joey managed to change the font size on his own computer and tried to convince Dalton to do the same. Dalton told Brianne, who knew that Joey would do something like that, so she double-checked his work on the computer monitor. Sure enough, her suspicions were confirmed. Joey printed a paper with two different font sizes. Brianne ordered Joey to turn off his computer and to go sit in the middle of the room.

Toby meanwhile managed to print three papers behind our backs. Brianne ordered Toby to go sit with Joey. We watched Dalton, who reciprocated with a glare. Dalton returned his focus to his assignment, because he remembered that he would lose his recess time if he did not do his work. Dalton usually only had one sentence typed by the time lab ended. Creative writing was an ongoing problem for Dalton, even more so than it was for the other deaf students.

As lunch approached, I prepared the students to line up. I felt a shout coming from a puff of air across my face. I looked at Dalton who angrily signed and yelled, "Lion!" He was pointing at the other students.

Confused, I signed, "Is he a lion?"

Irately, Dalton shrieked, "Yes!"

I quickly searched for a similar meaning to the word 'lion.' "Did you mean liar?" I asked.

He simultaneously signed 'lion' and hissed, "Yes! Liar!"

A facepalm moment.

The deaf students needed to improve their sign language and literacy skills. They were so behind linguistically that the speech therapy sessions hurt them more than helped them.

With regards to how their deaf voices sound to hearing people, deaf adults often had negative experiences with their speech therapists as children. Unable to make the correct sounds, they were frustrated, embarrassed, or both. Those who tried to learn to speak were often called a "Hearie" by their deaf peers (being called a 'hearie' in the Deaf community is the same as being called a traitor). Victimology is crazy.

Literacy skills should take precedence over speech therapies, especially with deaf children, so that they can leave high school as independent adults. The ability to use speech does not make a deaf adult independent. Speech skills and the use of one's cognitive faculties are two separate things.

During our lunch break in the teacher's lounge, Mrs. Feldman was upset that the principal had asked Mrs. Clark to evaluate her sign language skills. I nearly choked. Mrs. Feldman did not need a qualified signer to evaluate her — and Mrs. Clark was not qualified to make the evaluation. The extent of Mrs. Clark's knowledge of sign language was the manual alphabet, but she and Mrs. Feldman both got their fingers in knots when they tried to fingerspell. How was Mrs. Clark supposed to evaluate Mrs. Feldman if Mrs. Feldman signed and Mrs. Clark did not?

For some reason, the principal decided Mrs. Clark was qualified, simply because she could do the manual alphabet ... Mindboggling.

Friday, May 14

On Friday morning, we had an assembly in the gym. The mascot of the local minor league baseball team was the guest speaker.

During events like this, deaf people should be seated on the front row with the interpreter right in front of them. The Deaf row, as I call it. That is the least restrictive environment for the deaf person and the least distracting for the hearing people as well; the deaf person can see the interpreter clearly and the interpreter is not interfering with the program.

I noticed that Cassie and Lauren were both standing back against the wall while the mascot stood, pacing back and forth, close to the audience. Alyssa, Joey and Toby sat separately at the far left of the assembly, while the third through fifth grade students sat separately to the far right. Emma, Dalton, Eli, Mike and Timmy sat right in the middle, away from either of the other two groups.

They were so spread out because they were sitting with their hearing friends. They obviously could not see the interpreter because they kept wiggling around, trying to see past the mascot as he paced back and forth.

Later in the day, during computer lab, the students were assigned to write an essay about the guest speaker. I mentioned to the adults individually that the students could not see the interpreters during the assembly. In each instance I was told that it is the students' responsibility to listen or sit where they can see.

Personally, I would not have gotten up and moved. It would have attracted embarrassing attention. Having an entire group of people, from various parts of the room, get up and move around so that they could see an ill-placed interpreter would have been very distracting to the other people trying to enjoy the program.

"Excuse me, excuse me, excuse me — oops, sorry, I didn't mean to step on your foot — excuse me..." as an entire group of students squeezed their way through the audience to find a seat where they could see the interpreter.

Hearing students are not forced to move around to better seats, whereas the deaf students must choose between sitting with their friends and being able to see the interpreter.

The interpreters insisted that they did not want to restrict the deaf students from being able to sit with their hearing friends. If that was the case, there was nothing stopping the *hearing* students from sitting with their *deaf* friends in the Deaf row. As it was, the interpreters should have moved closer to the front row.

Monday, May 24

It was the last week of the school year. Michelle had been absent from school, and I was curious if anyone knew anything about it. Mrs. Jones signed while maintaining her bewildered grin:

> "I'm surprised you all did not know this. Last Friday night, Michelle accidentally set her house on fire while her father slept in the garage. Luckily, the damage was only done to her own bedroom."

> Several of the staff stopped talking and turned their heads in our direction. I sat there slack jawed. Mrs. Jones continued, "…but Michelle was afraid to go back into the house, so her family sent her to stay with her grandmother."

The unfortunate thing was that in order to explain to Michelle the consequences of setting her bedroom on fire, the communication had to be done in ASL. However, Michelle's mother had refused to learn sign language. She preferred the lip-reading method, but Michelle could not read lips.

Michelle was an intelligent and methodical child, but how was she supposed to know the consequences of her actions without communication? Forcing a 4-year-old child to read lips is like trying to force a toddler to read a newspaper. They need to acquire linguistic knowledge first, and then they can learn to do other things like read lips. How could lip reading supply information when language does not exist in the first place? How do language-less people get and express information if they are unable to hear or verbally speak?

It's quite simple: they need to communicate by using American Sign Language.

Summer Break

It was the beginning of summer vacation when I met with my friend Brenda at a local Deaf Club. I asked her about sending her son Ritch to Knight school so that he could be with his friend, Mike.

Brenda's face became long, and with a sad look she said that Mike's family moved to Idaho.

"At first, they visited Utah and Idaho, but the father favored Idaho. Mike's mom wanted to settle in Utah because she liked the deaf support service at the Utah School for the Deaf. His father disagreed and convinced her to move to Idaho because that is where his family lives. In reality, the school program in Idaho where Mike will go has a strong emphasis on CI support service and oralism exposure.

"Actually," she continued, "the school in Idaho is more of a propaganda program, like here and the majority of other mainstreamed programs. The stronger the emphasis on speech therapy and the CI program, the larger the number of students with CI and the more powerful the propaganda."

"Mike is on target with his hearing peers!" I said in shock.

Brenda nodded. "Now Mike is gone, and Ritch has lost his best and only friend…"

"Timmy has lost his best friend too. Now he is the only deaf child left in his grade level," I added. Michelle and Mike had been transferred out of state.

> "When all else is lost, the future still remains."
>
> *Christian N. Bovee*

THIRD SEASON

Monday, August 23, 2004

The first day of school was for teachers only, as a final planning day before students arrived. Kallie was a middle school interpreter transferred in to work with either Joey or Mrs. Smith. None of the Knight School interpreters were willing to work with Mrs. Smith because she eviscerated them. Carmen was not allowed to work with Mrs. Smith because Mrs. Smith refused to allow her in the classroom. Kallie, being new, did not know about Mrs. Smith.

As we sat around the table discussing our duties for the coming year, Mrs. Jones informed us that the principal and all of the D/HH teachers had agreed that it was imperative to rotate the interpreters. The basis for this decision was to prevent and manage conflicts. It had not yet been decided who would be primarily working with Joey — Kallie or Brianne.

Mrs. Jones gave me a copy of my daily schedule, which was another round of confusing schedule rotations. With this schedule paper in my hand, I also learned that Dalton had been transferred out of state.

Tuesday, August 24

Several of the deaf students' parents dropped off their children for the first day of school. Most of the deaf students' parents were not very involved; however, Joey's mother was an exception. She poked her head into Mrs. Jones' room to say hello to everyone before she walked her son upstairs to Mrs. Weaver's room.

Before she left, Joey's mother quickly glanced at the names in the students' outgoing box, but then she stopped. The room instantly became cold and lifeless. She looked at Mrs. Jones and said, "Dalton's name is not here."

"That's right," Mrs. Jones said guardedly.

"How come?" She probed.

We squirmed uncomfortably as Mrs. Jones replied, "Dalton moved away, and we miss him."

Joey's mother pursed her lips, and with tongue in cheek she grinned as she disappeared into the crowd with Joey. With Dalton and Joey's history of fighting, her reaction to Dalton moving away wasn't surprising.

"What was that all about?" Kallie inquired.

"Never mind her," Mrs. Jones said as she returned to the duty assignments.

Kallie and Brianne wondered who would be interpreting for Mrs. Smith's class and for Joey. "I don't know which class I will be interpreting for," Brianne said nervously.

"I prefer working with older students, but I wouldn't mind interpreting for Mrs. Smith's pre-k class if there are not too many of them," Kallie said, waving her hands as if she were trying to stop a moving train.

Almost on cue, Mrs. Smith entered the room and barked at Mrs. Jones, "I need to speak with you out in the hall."

Moments later, Mrs. Jones returned and announced that Brianne would be working in Mrs. Smith's room and that Kallie would be interpreting for Joey. Mrs. Smith had a strong preference for Brianne, and Brianne was the only interpreter from last year that Mrs. Smith had not yet scared off. Mrs. Smith also believed that Brianne exercised authoritative control over the students. In spite of Mrs. Jones' seniority, it had become obvious that, being the submissive one, she had very little say in which interpreter worked where.

Interpreter Carmen on the other hand had a bad habit of encroaching the students' personal space. She hovered over the children that she was interpreting for, which really aggravated them. To make matters worse, her signs were not very clear. She often incorrectly signed similar words, such as "Memory" (the open '5' hand pulling from the forehead and ending in a closed 'S' hand to indicate 'holding onto the thought') and "Guess" (the 'D' hand with the index finger pointing at the forehead and moving out in front of the forehead in the closed 'S' hand to indicate 'grasping at an idea').

This is why we needed a Deaf faculty member or a head interpreter to assess interpreters. Only a day into the new school year, and I was already being reminded of this.

Tuesday, September 7

Stewart, a struggling fifth grader, was standing by the cafeteria door crying. Mrs. Feldman walked by, and I asked her what had happened. Apparently, Stewart had lost his CI and had been unable to function without it.

The child could no longer use BTE hearing aids, because the CI surgery had destroyed all of his natural residual hearing. Even more disturbing, Stewart did not know any sign language. There was no backup support plan to accommodate him, and this was not the first time something like this had happened. An implanted child is still legally deaf, and they seemed to forget this fact themselves.

Stewart would not have had this problem if he were enrolled in the deaf classroom setting or at a Deaf school where only one language was used — or even if the school provided a back-up CI.

Stewart, with no way to communicate or learn, cried in the hallway, stood alone during recess, had panic attacks, and fidgeted a lot. Earlier in the year, Stewart had been sent to the principal's office for punching a boy in the face. That time also he didn't have his Cochlear Implant, and he had misunderstood the boy's comment about his CI. He was unable to deal with the language-less environment around him.

During recess, Mrs. Weaver approached me, pointing her finger directly in my face, asking me why I was wearing sunglasses. I flinched uncomfortably as she poked at the lens of my sunglasses.

"Because it is glaringly bright outside," I said, holding my hands up high to keep her fingers out of my face.

"Oh, I thought it was to protect your eyes so that Emma couldn't poke them," Mrs. Weaver said, still poking at my sunglasses. I got the feeling that she was trying to incite me.

* * *

Later that afternoon, in the teacher's lounge, I complained to Mrs. Feldman about Mrs. Weaver's behavior. Cassie seemed interested, but Mrs. Feldman just shrugged, so I digressed and commented that Mrs. Weaver hadn't been eating in the teachers' lounge lately.

"That's because she knows that she is hated," Mrs. Feldman said.

"Mrs. Weaver is very picky about the students in her class," Cassie said rather gossipy. "She prefers them white, rich, charismatic, and popular. If she gets a student who doesn't meet her taste, she calls them 'F-L-K'. Didn't you notice the black kid in her class who always has time-out during recess? Every day? It kinda makes you wonder..."

Confused, I asked, "What's F-L-K?"

"Funny Looking Kid," Cassie signed with a disapproving look on her face. "Mrs. Weaver has been in trouble for calling students that before."

Wednesday, September 17

It was school picture day. Several of the teachers and interpreters busted out laughing as I walked into the teachers' lounge to have my lunch.

"What's so funny?" I grinned.

Brianne straightened herself up, swallowed the food in her mouth and retold the story. "This is funny. The photographer told one of the deaf students to say cheese. So I signed to the student, 'Say cheese'."

The giggling adults fired up again while I waited for the punch line.

"OK, OK, the deaf student looked confused," Brianne giggled as the other adults howled again.

My stomach sank a bit.

Brianne collected herself enough to finish the story. "The deaf kid *signed* the word 'Cheese,' in the literal sense, like an actual cheese, instead of pronouncing the slang word, 'Cheese,' out loud."

Several of the adults busted out laughing again. "Totally inappropriate," I pretended to smile.

Young *deaf students* do not understand spoken idioms, phrases and *sound related* phonetic jokes. Their hearing families choose not to communicate with them the same way they do with their hearing children. If they communicated using ASL in conversational form, their deaf children would not be in these predicaments. However, hearing people often see it as something that any child would do.

Brianne should have known better too. She should have signed "Smile" instead of "Cheese".

Another interpreter jumped on the band wagon and told the group her story. "The photographer told a deaf third grader to say 'Pepsi'. He cried and said, "But...but...I don't like soda!"

Another round of laughter ensued, at the expense of deaf students.

It would have been more meaningful and educationally productive if the interpreters had taken the time to teach the children new things. After all, they were supposed to act as teacher's aides whenever possible. It just continued to look like "whenever possible" meant "whenever I feel like it" to far too many people.

Thursday, September 23

On Deaf Row

Mr. Paynes, the science teacher, had the desks in his classroom arranged in two columns and four rows. In each of the two columns, there were three or four desks in each row. I sat in the back row of the left column where the deaf students had assigned seats, their Deaf row.

Cassie typically stood near the blackboard, next to the front row, approximately 30 feet from the deaf students. It was tough to watch the interpreter from that distance. I asked her if the deaf students could move up to the front row and switch seats with some of the hearing students.

"I've already asked Mr. Paynes to do that in the past. Nothing was done. I guess he will never change." She shrugged and continued, "Maybe it is because most of them only come in the afternoons. I don't know."

87

When she finished talking to me, Cassie left the room. Mrs. Feldman came in and started interpreting for the deaf third graders. She briefly explained that Cassie had gone home sick and that she would be substituting for Cassie.

"Now a teacher for a change!" I thought. Surely she would be able to see how the deaf third graders learn and act in a hearing classroom.

Mr. Paynes started a science video about water. Mrs. Feldman started to sign. She was skipping points, and she mis-signed the word 'then' for the word 'than'. "60 melytr is more 'then' 40 miletr."

She had grammatical errors as well as her spelling errors for milliliter, which she spelled out as 'melytr' and 'miletr'. I groaned, dropped my head on Emma's desk.

According to studies, most deaf students leave high school with a third or fourth grade reading level. Day in and day out of these constantly mis-signed words and misuses of certain signed words was truly maddening.

I waited until a pause in the video before I asked Mrs. Feldman if she would turn on the closed captioning. It was my subtle way of trying to stop her from signing.

Mr. Paynes took the deaf students' microphones from his neck, turned them off, and placed them on his desk. Then he said something. I quickly looked at Mrs. Feldman to see what he had said, but she did not sign anything. I supposed that is must have been unimportant.

I looked at Alyssa. Alyssa watched Mrs. Feldman with intent focus even though she did not comprehend lip reading. Alyssa sat by her desk like the perfect little mannequin frozen in its place, looking like she'd been listening.

"What have you learned in here?" I casually asked her.

Alyssa looked at me with her green eyes wide, barely showing her perfect white teeth.

"Fine," she signed.

Her reply left me wondering if she meant that, or something else.

Seconds later, the hearing students got up and put their things into their desks and backpacks. I informed the deaf students that it was time to put away their books and start lining up. Mrs. Feldman must have missed Mr. Paynes' dismissal, because if I had not told them it was time to go, they would probably still be sitting there wondering why everyone else got up.

"They were waiting for me to dismiss them!" I thought to myself.

After the class, Mrs. Feldman came up to me and complained that Alyssa's reading and expression level were low. Mrs. Feldman had chosen not to listen to Mrs. Jones' input about Alyssa's consistent areas of concern. Now she saw for herself how deficient Alyssa was in her reading and writing skills.

Wednesday, October 6

It seemed that the month of October was the most fun month. That was when the deaf students excitedly chattered about Halloween costumes. It was the only time I saw lively, stimulating conversation happening among them.

I remembered Alyssa's struggle to tell me about shopping for shoes the previous year. This year was remarkably different. Alyssa ran up to me after recess before I walked into the building. I turned around and looked at Alyssa standing beside Cassie.

"Hi Alyssa!" I signed.

"She has something she wants to tell you, but I could not quite get what she was trying to say." Cassie signed, pointing to Alyssa. "Maybe you could help?"

I nodded wondering what Alyssa had to tell me.

Alyssa stood there beaming with a big smile. I read her lips as she spoke, "RT 'quitet'."

She fingerspelled, "C-C."

I glanced at Cassie as she fingerspelled 'quitet'.

I remembered Alyssa's spoken word for costume and said, "What kind of costume did you get?"

Alyssa signed this time. She made a left-handed manual 'Q' and tapped on her right shoulder, "RT 'quitet' costume."

"You spoke the word 'quitet'," I copied her signed word for 'quitet'. "What did you mean? Please explain the word 'quitet'."

Alyssa pondered and detailed her costume using gestural signs. She described an iconic shape of the dress that Cinderella wore, as if it was on her body.

Cassie and I looked at each other and suddenly figured out what she meant. Alyssa had used the manual letter, "Q" instead of "P." But while she hadn't really intended to speak "Puitet" for "Princess," either, it seemed she had been trying to tell us about being a princess, regardless of whether her assumed choice of correct words might also have been incorrect too, as she struggled to be 'heard' through her reading/speaking expressive communication disorder.

We simultaneously signed, "You mean 'Princess'?" and to confirm our guess, I made a 'P' hand-shape and moved the hand-shape from my left shoulder to my right hip, as if the princess wore a sash.

Alyssa nodded her head smiling.

I signed elaborately as if a hearing person were using a lilting tone, "Oh, you have a princess costume!"

Cassie and I smiled as Alyssa hugged us both.

Throughout the day, Toby consistently avoided wearing his tele-loop device. He got very embarrassed when he had to hand the AEA microphone to the special-related teachers. His demeanor changed every single time. He would try and find excuses to avoid having to do it.

"Wait. I don't want to interrupt the class."

"The battery is already dead."

Or he would conceal the tele-loop device from view and deliberately forget to hand it to the teacher.

* * *

Later that night, I emailed Angela. I asked her for professional feedback on how to deal with the student's refusal to wear the auditory trainers.

"Libby! You remember, we hated wearing them! You remember how hot and humid it was in Hattiesburg, when we had to wear those rubbery straps on our bare skin? The straps literally stuck to our necks and shoulders when we played outside. It was icky and uncomfortable to peel it off our skin before we went home after school."

She was right. The devices had felt like moistened lollipops stuck to our necks. I felt bad for Toby, but I still didn't have a solution for him, or for his behavior.

Monday, October 11

I met Brianne in the teachers' lounge and asked her how she liked working with Mrs. Smith.

"It's not that bad now. She has easier students this year," she said.

"Are you implying that it is because Eli isn't in her class?" I asked.

Brianne casually signed with one hand, "Yeah, that's probably why."

Cassie waited for Brianne to leave the room before informing me that Brianne's attitude was becoming more like Mrs. Smith's. I groaned. It was too bad that Brianne ended up being sucked into Mrs. Smith's victim-blaming psyche.

Cassie mentioned that she had noticed that Mrs. Jones was not working with Emma as much this year as she had last year. I said that it was true. I could see why Mrs. Jones had partially given up on Emma.

Last year, Mrs. Jones had put a lot of effort into helping Emma memorize addition and subtraction equations, but she would forget them within minutes. This year, teaching Emma would need to learn better numerical management skills, making sure she knew how to add and take away without using objects or her fingers. She left Emma under my care most of the day this year.

"I noticed that Mrs. Jones often goes over to observe the three deaf kindergarteners in the integrated kindergarten classroom rather than coming to observe Emma with you there. I am not a certified D/HH teacher, but I feel that Emma should not be under your direct care all day," Cassie said.

Later, while the students were outside for recess, Joey was leaning up against a metal fence post. The magnetic piece of his CI leapt off his head onto the metal post as he leaned back against the pole. It was a sight to see. I tried not to stare as he grappled with the device, trying to get it back on his head. I looked around to see if any of the other students saw what happened. They did not. I was relieved for him.

I crept up to him and casually signed, "What are you doing here?"

He said something in a meek tone.

"Please sign because I am unable to read your lips," I said.

"I have a time out."

I felt it was a perfect time to talk about something else. "How do you like being in Mrs. Weaver's classroom?" I asked.

"I want to be with my friends from last year," he replied.

"You mean you want to be with Alyssa, Toby... and all the other deaf students?"

"Yes," he nodded, looking away.

"Well, you have your own interpreter. Interpreter Kallie is new. You're lucky," I said, trying to encourage him.

He said that he did not understand her signs and that he preferred Mrs. Jones.

"You should tell your parents. Beg if you have to," I suggested, trying to empower him.

If he only knew what his options and rights were, he could have chosen differently. But, even if his parents allowed him to choose, he probably would have picked whichever he thought would please them anyway.

Just before school was over for the day, the fire department came out to give a demonstration on the black top behind the school. The third graders came out to look at the fire truck as the instructor lectured about safety. I watched Kallie interpret in SEE 2.

"Be keep if you breathe eat in the space, if you went leave and with your mom and mom," she signed using perfect SEE 2 signs, but signing the wrong words.

I translated her mis-signs in my head, which should have said, "Be careful not to breathe the smoke in the air, just go out and meet your mom and dad."

Tuesday, October 12 – Friday, October 15

When I walked into the classroom, I saw a note on the desk:

"I will be gone for several days due to a death in the family. I am not sure who the interpreter will be. I tried to get Mrs. Miller, but she was already substituting for someone else. See you later, Mrs. Jones."

Mr. Grant was the substitute for Mrs. Jones. He constantly disregarded my request for him to leave Emma alone. He prevented her from taking her daily nap, which clearly violated her IEP agreement. I told him repeatedly that Emma required a daily nap.

He also disregarded my request to leave the students in the classroom until the exact time to leave. He rounded them up and did not make them line up when leaving the classroom. Mr. Grant created disorder and chaos for the deaf students. The deaf students looked up to him knowing full well that Mrs. Jones, the interpreters, and I did not approve of this.

Emma's IEP specifically stated that she must have one-on-one assistance all day. Timmy, on the other hand, could not lip read, so he needed an interpreter all day, especially during math. Mrs. Jones had explicitly explained this on the note for Mr. Grant. Donna was Timmy's interpreter, and Mr. Grant was supposed to accompany Emma to one of her special-related classes. Instead, he ordered Donna to go with Emma to the special-related class — while he stayed in the classroom to teach Timmy. This was a complete violation of the IEP because Timmy was entirely dependent on an interpreter.

Since one of the interpreters, Jayme, had quit, one of the other interpreters, Misty, had stayed in our classroom during her breaks.

Misty's presence clearly enticed Mr. Grant. Every day, he showed up wearing over-powering cologne, flirted with her, and allowed the deaf students to leave the class early for lunch, special-related classes and recess, so that he could have time alone with her. Every day, his behavior became more obvious. He certainly did not seem to have the best interest of the students in mind.

* * *

Mrs. Jones came back a week later. She gathered the students on the floor for community circle time. She asked how the students liked the substitute. Emma and Toby hollered that they liked him. Timmy responded with mixed signs in SEE 2 and ASL, "No! He talk same duck."

I looked at Mrs. Jones' baffled expression.

"What do you mean Mr. Grant talked like a duck?" She asked.

Timmy was at a loss for words and could not explain what he meant.

"His voice sounded like a duck, very low and rough sounding," I tried to help him clarify.

Mrs. Jones made a gross facial expression. I could not help it myself; I snickered.

"I not understand his talk," Timmy added in mixed SEE 2 and ASL, "I say him I like Interpreter Pamela help with me math."

I explained that Mr. Grant had made Donna go with Emma.

"That wasn't what I told him!" Mrs. Jones was aghast. "I wrote the details down for him! Timmy doesn't understand anything without an interpreter!"

"Yeah, Libby and I both tried to tell him that," Donna spoke up.

Mrs. Jones sat on the floor shaking her head for an uncomfortably long while.

94

Saturday, October 16

The third Saturday of the month was when the members of the Deaf Club hosted meetings and social events. This event was unique because the local Deaf Club threw a Halloween party. Blossom and Paxton, two of the other deaf students from Knight school, came to the Deaf Club. Eli arrived later that evening. It was such a delight to socialize with the CODA kids (hearing Children of Deaf Adults). They signed and communicated without any stigma attached.

I bumped into Blossom's mom, Junie, while she stood in line to pay her Deaf Club fee. She told me that she felt like something was wrong with Mrs. Smith's demeanor. Junie complained that Mrs. Smith was moody all the time and constantly blamed it on the deaf students.

I spotted an acquaintance named Chad at the party. I pointed out Chad to Junie and told her that he was the father of Deaf twin boys and that Knight wanted them. Junie motioned to me, pointing at Chad.

I turned to look at Chad and he signed to me with a stern facial expression, "Never will send my Deaf boys to Knight! Never!"

I did not realize that he had such as strong opposition to Knight before this. I turned back toward Junie who was echoing Chad's words, "Never."

Chad went on to defend his reasons for feeling this way, holding a toddler in each arm. He was opposed to their SEE 2 philosophy. He wanted his boys to be taught in their native language, ASL.

"Well, educationally, it's best if your sons receive early childhood exposure to signing, as soon as possible, regardless of the communication method," I said.

"I am very aware of that, which is why we will meet with the Area Education Agency next week," he signed. "I will request them to find a qualified ASL teacher to teach my boys. Their first language is ASL! I do not support oralism!"

Junie jumped in, "Yes, I agree! My daughter is talking a lot and not signing at all. I do not understand one word. It was easier to understand her when she signed, but I don't know why she quit signing!"

I looked at Blossom and signed to her, but I was interrupted by her chattering mouth, which made no sense to any of us. Blossom wanted so much to share whatever she saw or what was on her mind. Junie and I looked at each other and helplessly shrugged, not understanding what her daughter had just said.

Later that evening, I discussed this conversation with a deaf acquaintance, Saffiyah. I pointed out that the school does not have the money to support extra faculty for just the deaf children of parents who used ASL at home: Blossom, Eli and the twins if they came.

"I wouldn't be surprised if AEA told Chad and Lisa to send the boys to Deaf School," she interjected. "Financially, it would save the school money to send the child to wherever there is Deaf culture and ASL support, rather than providing support, when there was one already established elsewhere."

I had to agree with her because it made a lot of sense.

Thursday, October 21

It was the first day of National Standardized Testing (NST), and Mrs. Jones explained to the edgy third graders that they would be tested every day for one or two weeks. She detailed how hard the test would be and that they had to do their best.

Emma arrived at school with her prescription glasses smashed up. She broke them on her way to school in the AEA-assigned special education transportation van. She broke them in order to get out of doing the NST.

I was relieved when the van was provided for Emma, rather than the short yellow school bus. A lot of the deaf bus riders were branded for being in the short yellow school bus with other riders with multi-disabilities. The AEA van was a nice upgrade, yet somewhat discreet. But that didn't hide the fact that lots of these deaf riders spent up to an hour in these transportation vans one way ... *alone*.

During the NST, there were many adults interrupting the classroom; notoriously, Kallie and the speech therapists. I suggested that Mrs. Jones put up a sign, but she rejected my suggestion because several of the support staff needed to see her often. Mrs. Feldman put up such a sign on her door though.

Emma lacked fine motor skills, which created a problem for her during the test. It was difficult for her to fill in the little dots on the paper with a number two pencil. She pressed the pencil too hard and marked all over the page. I asked Mrs. Jones if Emma could use her finger to point to her answer and I mark it down for her. Mrs. Jones said that she had checked with the school counselor beforehand, but the counselor said that school policy forbade teachers saying the options aloud, and I could not mark down Emma's best pick.

"This isn't an equal access," I thought to myself. "I don't know whether it's the school policy or the NST policy, but it clearly wasn't written with the welfare of any of the Deaf or otherwise cognitively disabled students in mind." This policy clearly needs to be revisited.

Later that day, Mrs. Jones told me that neither Emma nor Toby did well on the test. I inquired about Emma and Toby's reading skills, especially when it came to them being able to read the questions on the test. Mrs. Jones was at a loss for words to explain their low scores. Naturally, their scores were not satisfactory, and Mrs. Jones did not want their parents to feel overwhelmed by their children's low scores on the test.

Mrs. Jones had an idea. She asked me and the reading volunteer to watch the students while she went to the lab and made copies of Emma and Toby's NST answer sheets. When she returned, she took one student at a time and tested them orally. Mrs. Jones explained to me and the reading volunteer that what she was doing was not permissible and that she was only doing this for her own benefit and for their parents' knowledge.

Mrs. Jones covered the student's answer sheets with her hand to keep the students from looking at the sheet and repeating their previous answers. She had me and the reading volunteer sit with one of the students and sign the questions. When she was finished, she switched students, repeating the process with each one. As a result of using this unconventional method, the students scored much higher; high enough to make a statistical difference.

I imagined that the parents were ecstatic with their children's test scores using the spoken method. Sadly, the scores could not be used for the official record because the written test had already been marked.

* * *

Interpreter Kallie walked into the room with Joey so that he could take the NST. Joey's IEP required him to have a longer time to respond to each question and to provide him with a less distracting environment. Kallie walked straight to the computer and browsed the web, while Emma and Toby were taking their NST. Mrs. Jones asked all of the room helpers to stand by and help interpret for her.

After constant distractions among the deaf students, I decided to put a portable partition between Emma and Toby, while keeping Joey in the far back of the room. I sat with Emma on the right side of Mrs. Jones, while Toby sat on her left behind the partition. Mrs. Jones sat three feet away, in front of all three of us. Kallie sat at a computer desk directly behind Mrs. Jones.

From behind Mrs. Jones, Kallie waved in my direction to get my attention. Emma and Toby looked up to watch Kallie's conversation with me. Mrs. Jones was so focused on reading the directions to the students that she didn't notice that they were not paying attention to her.

I warned Kallie that this was neither the time nor the place for casual conversation. The two students were very easily distracted, and there Kallie was, smiling, surfing the net, and drinking her 32-ounce soda. When she was finished with the computer, she got up and walked over to talk to Joey without asking Mrs. Jones if she needed help or if Joey was finished with the test.

Joey finished his test before his time was up.

Mrs. Jones signed directly to me that she believed Joey had hurried up without reading the questions and answers thoroughly.

Mrs. Jones startled me, "Oh! The counselor wants you to erase the excess markings and smudges off of Emma's answer sheet!"

I could not believe the logistics of this situation. Mrs. Jones took Emma while I erased the excess markings.

Emma broke another pair of her prescription glasses during her lunch break. She had several pairs of back-up glasses because of her tendency to break them, especially when she felt stressed out - in spite of all the "accommodations."

This is the Least Restrictive Environment policy in full effect. These two words chimed in my head, *Maximum extent.* Sometimes, that "Least Restrictive" mandate can be taken too far – into absurdity.

Tuesday, November 2

Timmy wanted my help with his assignments. He consistently refused to work alone and always asked an adult to help him get the right answers. He wanted perfect scores, but I suspect that he craved the real conversation and attention that he lacked at home and in the hearing classes. Either way, the program was not working on his side. To provide the stimulating conversation that he lacked, I found it easier to explain what he was supposed to do with his assignment through communication in ASL.

I looked over the reading and writing assignments for today, and it dawned on me that I had overlooked what kind of assignment it was. The assignments that were given to the deaf students consisted of sounding words, such as phonetics. This particular phonetic reading and writing material was "John and His Drum." I proceed to read the question on the assignment sheet, "Mark the vowel sound in each word: long, short, or r-controlled." There was no way that Timmy and Alyssa could have passed phonetics!

During my lunch break, I walked into the teachers' lounge and noticed everyone was chattering about something. I asked them what the news was.

Mrs. Feldman took a bite of her chocolate chip cookie and signed, "Josiah, the new fifth grade boy, can hear now! He does not need interpreter service, and he will go back to his home school district! The audiologist said that Josiah's hearing has improved slightly."

Puzzled, I asked for more information, "What do you mean he can hear now?"

It is completely unheard of for someone to miraculously regain one of the five senses without medical intervention, usually requiring surgical intervention.

Mrs. Feldman explained that the family had taken Josiah to their church on a weekly basis to pray over his ears to prevent him from losing more of his hearing. Josiah's reading level had dropped because of his slow but progressive hearing loss. The pastor had popped Josiah's ears and now he could hear.

"Isn't it amazing?!" Mrs. Feldman interpreted for one of the teachers. I did not know which teacher had said it.

In shock, I spoke and signed simultaneously:

"That is cruel! Having your ears popped does hurt!"

The teachers, including Mrs. Feldman, ignored me, continuing to praise God for restoring Josiah's hearing.

Unable to eat my lunch after that, I looked on in dismay. Still reeling in disbelief, I made a doubtful facial expression at Cassie and signed, "Really?"

She nodded at me discreetly.

I simultaneously signed and spoke, "That's what the family thinks. I think the pastor just temporarily readjusted the inner ear anatomy and that is what enabled Josiah to hear briefly."

Mrs. Feldman continued to speak highly of the incident.

"Well, I can hear better after my ears pop when the plane takes off and my hearing returns to normal after the plane lands. Basically, I think that's what happened to Josiah," Cassie signed.

Mrs. Feldman started to debunk Cassie's theory, but Cassie interrupted her remembering something she had seen.

"Yesterday morning, right after he got off the bus, I saw Josiah put his thumb in his mouth and he blew hard enough to make his cheeks puff out. That can temporarily restore his hearing until the pressure in his ears returns to normal. I think Josiah is tricking his parents, giving them a false sense of hope so that he can go back to his home school district. Don't you remember telling me how much he missed his old school? Or maybe he's trying to appease his disappointed parents for being 'deaf'." She made quotation marks with her fingers and finished the sentence with ASL slang for, "You know?"

I nodded in acknowledgment, but Mrs. Feldman shrugged.

Thursday, November 11

Later that morning, I walked into the teachers' lounge. Mrs. Feldman, Brianne and Cassie were talking, when Mrs. Feldman slammed her fist into the table. I asked Mrs. Feldman if she was OK.

"No. Josiah has lost his hearing again. The audiologist retested him a week later, and his hearing is the same as it was before the pastor popped Josiah's ears!" She scowled.

"Are you upset that Josiah is now deaf again?" I asked.

"No, not really; it's just the excitement of a miracle that didn't permanently stay that bugs me." (She signed 'bug' in the noun sense meaning 'insect' rather than the transitive verb for the synonymous word 'bother.')

I looked at Cassie who observed the situation. She shrugged and grinned. My point was made that there was never any miracle.

The conversation shifted to Alyssa. Mrs. Feldman signed Alyssa's name as the word 'menstruation', with the manual letter 'A' gently tapping on the cheek several times. Alyssa's name sign was similar, with the hand positioned differently, pressing the thumb on the cheek, then twist the manual letter 'A'. I kept telling Mrs. Feldman that Alyssa's name sign was not 'menstruation', but Mrs. Feldman replied:

"I know but I find that easier to use."

In such disbelief, I looked at the interpreters who cocked their eyebrows as if to say that they agreed that Mrs. Feldman was wrong for doing that. Cassie decided to tell her to quit using such an embarrassing sign for Alyssa's name. Mrs. Feldman looked at her and agreed to not use this 'menstruation' name sign anymore.

Why did Mrs. Feldman listen to a hearing woman, but not to me? "Oh come on," I snapped.

Later, I found out why Mrs. Feldman seemed to be irrational: She was pregnant. It wasn't an excuse for embarrassing Alyssa, but at least I was able to give Mrs. Feldman some slack for her emotional outbursts.

Friday, November 12

Mrs. Miller informed me that Mrs. Smith was not using sign language in the classroom. Cassie confirmed the allegation, saying that Mrs. Smith never signed when she interpreted for her class either.

I told them that Junie could not understand her daughter Blossom's speech, and that Blossom had not been using as much sign as she previously did.

"It's Blossom's choice to use speech and not sign language," Brianne interrupted.

"Now why is that?" I asked.

"Well, Blossom sees her classmates using speech, and none of them use sign. Maybe that's what encourages her, or motivates her, to use speech," Brianne retorted.

"Well, Blossom's mom does not understand her anymore. She understood her just fine when she was using sign language," I said.

"Too bad for Mom," Brianne said. "She has to accept Blossom's decision. Sign language is a minority in her classroom."

I watched Brianne with revulsion as she continued, "She's constantly exposed to speech. Her deaf friend, Sidda, also talks and doesn't sign."

Cassie seemed to be as turned off by this as I was. We left the teachers' lounge together.

"Blossom does too need to use sign!" Cassie said after we left. "Her speech is unintelligible, like Timmy's and Alyssa's. The only way for people to understand her is through her use of signs, and you know damned well how clearly she communicated with them!"

After lunch, I informed Mrs. Miller what Brianne had said. She shook her head and said, "LRE should be more than just 'Least

Restrictive Environment'; it should be 'Language en-Riched Environment'. A classroom that uses sign language at all times is the basis of a least restrictive environment. Deaf students being in an inclusive program is not a least restrictive environment, because language, communication and spontaneous interaction are absent – think of that feral child, Genie."

Mrs. Miller continued to sign, "Do you want to know what Mrs. Smith said yesterday afternoon?"

"What?" I curiously replied.

Mrs. Miller revealed that Mrs. Smith asked Brianne to do the assessments on pre-kindergarten deaf children right in front of her.

Mrs. Miller became visibly upset, because she had her BA degree in Elementary Education, and she was the full-time substitute teacher. Brianne was a teenage mom with an education that fulfilled the requirements to interpret. She had no credentials or training to perform the assessments for the report cards.

Mrs. Miller reported this to the principal. In her complaint, Mrs. Miller stated she used sign language and needed Brianne's help to hold the books while she signed to the little deaf students.

Wednesday, November 17

It was nearing Thanksgiving break. I arrived to school late. As I walked toward Mrs. Jones' room, I spotted Carmen walking out. The students and interpreters were not supposed to be in Mrs. Jones' classroom for another 10 minutes. I was puzzled.

"Is there anything wrong with Emma? Why is Emma here early?"

"The music teacher was fussing at the students for behaving badly. I thought Emma was exceptionally wonderful, so I told her that we could leave the music room early," Carmen stammered.

I expressed my disagreement, "Emma needs to stay with her peers in order to learn the social norms of identifying the difference between right and wrong. She needs to know that teachers fuss at hearing students and that she was great today — something to make Emma think for herself. I always make Emma stay in her classes

103

until her homeroom teacher retrieves her. I make Emma stay in line with the rest of her class. Next time, be sure to keep Emma with her peers, okay?"

Carmen mumbled something and left.

Shortly after that, the entire D/HH support staff filed into Mrs. Jones' room with the deaf students. Unbeknownst to me, the support staff had agreed beforehand to give up their lunch break to show the meaning of thanks in the spirit of Thanksgiving. They planned to have a Thanksgiving feast in Mrs. Jones' room and had cooked copious amounts of Thanksgiving food.

All the Knight Elementary deaf students mingled in the classroom until Carmen began to verbally narrate a story from a book, giving the staff time to set up a buffet table. No other interpreter was provided, and Carmen did not sign while she read – so she should have signed or asked someone else to interpret. When the story telling had ended, the staff told the students to go wash their hands.

The older deaf students helped the younger students carry their trays of food. I stood by the table while the students got their food. Each of them grunted as they pointed at the different foods. I noticed that the speech therapist was there, instructing the students on how to say certain phrases like, "I want mashed potatoes," or "May I have more carrots?" The speech therapist wanted them to speak aloud instead of using their hands to point at the food, and she inadvertently stopped them from using ASL pronominalization. My eyes popped out when I saw her ask one of the students, "Do you want on state?"

I waited until the students were finished before asking her what, "On state," meant.

"Onion," she mouthed the word.

I was becoming vexed. "Show me this (I demonstrated the sign for 'state')."

"That's the suffix of 'I-O-N'," she fingerspelled the last three letters.

The speech therapist had signed the word 'onion' incorrectly by applying SEE 1 method, and this was due to the school's SEE 2 policy.

The D/HH teachers, interpreters, and support staff used the signs for 'On' and '-ION' instead. All of the D/HH staff used the SEE 1 method nearly all the time without realizing it, just as any native signer reverts to sign language when the hearing staff aren't watching.

The word 'On' is signed as if something is placed on top of something — 'On.' Then the morpheme of '-ION' (which is a noun suffix for "The act of doing something") is placed at the end of the word. It makes no sense to say, "Do you want 'ON + ION' with your hamburger?" The SEE 2 and the ASL sign for "Onion," is the bent finger at the corner of the eye to act as if drying a teary eye.

I couldn't get over it. The speech therapist was literally ruining the Thanksgiving party for these students. The students squirmed in line, hungry and cranky, because they failed to articulate their speech perfectly. But it was better than having no Thanksgiving celebration at all.

Mrs. Miller walked into the classroom, looked at the food, and asked me which I had cooked.

I shook my head and signed, "They didn't ask me to cook or to bring anything. I wasn't aware of this event until about an hour ago."

Mrs. Miller's eyes widened, "They didn't include me either."

"And this is an all-inclusive program, they say?" I laughed.

We nodded our heads speechlessly, wondering why we had been excluded. All of the adults ate with the students. Lauren and I then sat together.

"Doesn't this food look whole some?" she commented.

I was confused. Was the food 'whole' or was it 'some'?

I asked her to clarify what she meant. I nearly choked on my food at her explanation. She was using the SEE 1 applied method for 'whole' and 'some'. The signs were actually intended in the adjective sense of 'wholesome'.

The party was over and we were cleaning up. Carmen was due to interpret for the fourth grade class, which had three deaf students. Two of the three were dependent upon interpreter service. Carmen, whose regularly scheduled lunch break should have been long over, told Mrs. Feldman that she was going on her lunch break.

"Wait a minute! You just had your lunch break with us! You have students waiting for you!" Mrs. Feldman objected.

"My lunch break means having lunch without sitting down with students. My lunch break is away from the students. My lunch break equals cigarette break. I did not have any of those," Carmen replied sarcastically, waving a pack of cigarettes in her hand.

When Carmen saw Mrs. Feldman's face, she relented, "OK, I'll take my break 30 minutes before school is out, during the last period."

"What about Allen, Rachel and Zeke in their last period? They need an interpreted service," Mrs. Feldman insisted.

"You pick which break I take. I'm still following my contract," Carmen quipped and walked out of the room.

"What break?" I asked Mrs. Feldman.

"I believe the government law requires a 15-minute break every four hours," Mrs. Feldman explained.

"So I'm supposed to have a break?" I asked, unsure of whether I was supposed to take a break or not.

Mrs. Feldman nodded in affirmation.

"Mrs. Jones never informed me of that," I said, remembering all of those times that I felt I could have used a break but worked right through.

"You must take a break and you should use it," Mrs. Feldman said.

How was I supposed to respond to this?

Friday, November 19

Later that week, the principal announced budget cuts. He reduced three associates' hours. After the initial budget cut, the principal called a staff meeting to find more ways to save money or to lay off more associates. Cassie was the interpreter at the meeting. She and I sat at the same table.

It was an emotionally charged meeting.

"Send the students home 30 minutes earlier each day," one teacher suggested.

"Merge the deaf program from pre-k through fifth grade into one classroom and have just one teacher," another teacher said.

Several adults yelled, "That's not possible!"

I turned to see who was opposing the idea. It was the D/HH staff and interpreters.

"As I have stated before, merging the D/HH programs is not an option," the principle announced. "Any other ideas?"

"Yes, since you cut three other associate's hours, you may as well cut Libby's hours too," the music teacher said. "Emma takes her naps and several interpreters could rotate their schedules to assist her needs; they have one hour of flex time."

I gasped. Several of my co-workers supported me. "I refuse to take her job! I'll quit this instant if I'm assigned to work with that special needs girl."

"Libby has been a godsend, and she's done wonders with Emma. I want her to stay here," the art teacher spoke up.

"She's covered by the special education budget so she stays," Mrs. Jones defended. "She's what the deaf students need – a role model."

I breathed a sigh of relief. Mrs. Jones was right.

Wednesday, December 8

Joey's parents visited with Mrs. Jones. I waited until his parents left to ask her about the reason for the visit.

"Joey's parents grumbled when I told them that Joey was not listening to directions. They thought the classroom had too much sound interference like echoes, scuffing on the floor, students talking, and a lot of background noise."

"But Joey has never listened ever since he was in kindergarten, he simply doesn't know how." I bluntly replied.

"Right, and the parents are blaming the school system. They even hired a sound technician from the local school district. The sound technician said that the sounds were normal and consistent with all the other classrooms at all the different schools. There is no evidence of noise pollution." Mrs. Jones said.

Mrs. Jones added that Mrs. Weaver had a voice that carried over the classroom very well. I accidentally laughed out loud. A voice that carries over the room was no definite solution.

At Deaf school, if the teacher signed, it was almost a guarantee that the students would pay attention. They knew that if they looked away, even for a moment, they would lose a lot of vital information. It was basic common sense — so basic that even the preschoolers from the Deaf school picked up on it, especially if their parents communicated with them in sign at home. Enforcing the use of voice and hearing aids only took away from their receptive skills.

The deaf students at Knight School chatted a lot in class, unknowingly using ASL as their main choice of communication. Clearly, the school's preferred SEE2 communication method policy should have been reexamined.

Wednesday, December 15

The school board claimed to have a list of back-up interpreters, but none of the Knight School interpreters were ever substituted by the back-up interpreters. If they were absent, the only people left to serve as interpreters were the D/HH teachers (except Mrs. Smith, because she insists she's only a teacher, not an interpreter), and the three remaining interpreters. And just recently, three interpreters called out sick.

The school had an indoor recess because of stormy weather. The deaf and the hearing third graders, Cassie and I spent the time in one of the two third-grade teachers, Mr. Paynes' classroom.

Mr. Paynes initiated a game and explained the rules.

"Everyone sit on your desk Indian style. No kneeling or touching the floor with your feet. Bottoms sit firmly on the desk. Now, a girl cannot throw the ball to a girl and a boy cannot throw the ball to a boy. A column of desks cannot throw the ball within the same column. A row cannot throw within the same row.

Everything is done in the opposite. The ball cannot stay in your hands for more than three seconds. The ball cannot bounce out of your hands. You cannot throw the ball back to the person who threw it to you. If any of the rules is broken, the person has to sit down on the chair. The game ends in two minutes and the players remaining on the desks will receive snacks. Then we will play again. Everyone understand?"

All of the hearing students nodded their heads in affirmation. The deaf students sat there not reciprocating affirmative responses.

Mr. Paynes tossed the ball to a hearing student in the front row and blew a whistle. I watched the students toss the ball around, not once throwing it to a deaf student. Perhaps it was because they were placed in the back corner in positions difficult to reach. One by one, all of the hearing students were eliminated. All four of the deaf students and one hearing student remained on their desks.

Mr. Paynes called the five students remaining on their desks up to the front to get their rewards. The hearing children groaned and grumbled as the winners were called up. The irony is that the hearing students never threw the ball to the deaf students. The game was played again with the same results.

If the hearing students did not want the deaf students to win, they should have taken a chance and thrown them the ball. For my part, I was glad they got a chance to be the winners for a change.

Monday, December 20

It was the last day in December before the winter break. During the last 30 minutes of the afternoon, Mr. Paynes and the third grade class had a winter party. He called upon the students to line up for food and drinks. Cassie barged in the room so abruptly that it startled me.

Seeing the expressions on my face, Cassie said, "Joey... you won't believe this..."

She composed herself and continued, "Do you know his mom very well?"

"Yes, last year when Joey was in second grade. What happened?" I asked curiously.

"Mrs. Weaver, in the hearing classroom, was giving out winter party presents to her students. The only deaf kid in the class is Joey. They brought something like cookies and drinks for everyone. As soon as Joey arrived at his desk to eat, the intercom beeped and announced, 'Joey, your speech van driver is here. It's time for you to go'."

Joey complained that he wanted to stay and celebrate.

Mrs. Weaver asked, "Did you talk to your parents about this, or reschedule the speech therapy?"

"She said it out loud! Joey's eyes welled up with tears, and he slammed his fist down on the desk. He left abruptly." Cassie finished.

"As if he has serious speech problems!" I exclaimed in disbelief. (Joey is the *least*-likely student to be misunderstood).

"Joey's mom should have changed the appointment date but chose not to… or she forgot about it… or the speech clinic did not allow rescheduling at the last minute since it was close to the holiday," Cassie finished, feeling disgusted.

I shook my head in dismay.

"What's worse, the secretary made that announcement over the intercom and the entire classroom heard it. It profoundly enforces their pre-existing negative stereotypical views. She should have been more discreet about it." Cassie added.

"By deafness one gains in one respect more than one loses; one misses more nonsense than sense."

Horace Walpole

FOURTH SEASON

Tuesday, January 4, 2005

Winter break was over and the New Year had begun. The morning of the first school day in January, Mrs. Jones informed me that I would be taking the deaf students to the cafeteria for violin lessons, every Tuesday at 9:30 AM, after the special-related classes. All other rooms were booked, so the cafeteria was the only available spot. I looked at her.

"I remember seeing the third graders practicing on violins in the cafeteria last year. Is that the same violin lessons for the deaf students now?" I asked.

"Yes. The violin lessons will last six weeks, I think," she said.

I tried to suppress my laughter at this facade and the lame attempt of 'hearifying' the deaf students. But as strange as it sounds, the deaf students were actually looking forward to the lessons.

"Then the third grade students will invite their parents to observe them on the sixth week," Mrs. Jones continued.

The deaf students were excited about the violin lessons. But they really needed more language support at school and at home. However, the more I visualized the deaf students playing violin, the more I considered the possibility that they might play beautifully.

Wednesday, January 5

I met with Mrs. Feldman in her classroom while the speech therapist was in the room spending time with the deaf third through fifth graders. This was scheduled for them every Wednesday from 9 to 9:30 A.M.

111

All of the interpreters pulled up chairs and gathered around in a mini-circle. I asked Mrs. Feldman about Josiah's hearing status.

"His hearing has remained stable since the pastor popped his ears, but the horrible thing is that his parents told him that he will be completely hearing by the time that he is finished with high school," she replied.

I shook my head in disbelief. Mrs. Feldman made a comment about deaf students being sent to Knight as a last resort. I disagreed and said that when the mainstream programs fail deaf students, they are sent to Deaf schools as a last resort. Mrs. Feldman acceded.

By the time they reach high school, deaf individuals' educational and social developments are delayed so much that it is almost beyond repair, because they have such a loss of fluency in ASL and written English, a loss of culture and a loss of identity.

None of the hearing administrators from their AEAs seemed to understand the magnitude of the social implications thrust upon the isolated deaf student. There were only two possible outcomes, as I had noticed, following three hierarchal common scenarios:

Firstly, the only deaf student in an all hearing school with no interpreter service or support service usually transfers to a hearing school that has a D/HH program. Isolated deaf students fail academically and socially at a school for all hearing students.

Secondly, deaf students may manage enough success in the D/HH program to get by, but this is less common. A student who is failing the D/HH program is usually sent to the Deaf school.

Thirdly, the final scenario is the deaf student who has failed both the hearing program and the D/HH program, he or she now struggles to fit into the Deaf school, both academically and socially.

The deaf student who is sent to an all-Deaf school from an all-hearing school is often overshadowed by the ASL language-rich deaf students. The language-deficient deaf student does not do well socially or academically because their language skills differ too greatly. They don't blend in unless they act fast to increase their language skills.

So the isolated deaf student either fails in both the hearing and the Deaf worlds, or he or she falls into the arms of the Deaf world. The isolated deaf student may adopt ASL as an exclusive language. He or she may grow up to marry a Deaf person. The student may even possibly put '*Deaf life*' first before his or her hearing family members.

The second scenario is exactly what the hearing world is trying to downplay; deaf students "falling beneath". On the other hand, in Deaf World, less social communication is 'Home Sweet Home' – *status quo*.

* * *

Emma was taking her daily nap after recess. Mrs. Miller and I sat talking about the discrimination, racism and prejudice at Knight. I told her about the job interview with my Deaf sister and the principal. Mrs. Miller's eyes widened. She asked me when my sister had sent in her application.

I thought about it and signed, "Spring of 2002. Why?"

Mrs. Miller tensed her lips, jerked her head left then right, then she slapped her thigh and buried her face in her hands.

I tapped her on the knee. "Why? Is there something that I don't know?"

"Did you know that there was a long-term substitute teacher for the third through fifth grade deaf students? In the fall of 2001, Mrs. Feldman was an interpreter. She had just graduated with an Associate of Arts in Interpreter training, and she was a student earning her bachelor degree in Elementary Education."

I became confused and did not make the connection until Mrs. Miller continued:

"I applied for that job too! I graduated with a bachelor's degree in Elementary Education in 1999. Ever since, I have been unable to find a full-time teaching position. Knight calls itself the most diversified school. What a joke! What's more, the state's Department of Education complains that it does not have enough minority teachers. Look at me. I am a black Deaf woman. Knight hired Mrs. Feldman in 2002, a white hearing woman, over your Deaf sister and me."

113

Dumbfounded, I leaned back in my chair and closed my eyes. I was simply stunned. The deaf students had a substitute teacher with no knowledge of Deaf Education, who was also an interpreter for one full year. Knight knew full well that there were qualified teachers out there!

Mrs. Miller startled me as she bent over close to my right side and gently signed to someone behind me.

"Tap Libby on the shoulder," she signed. "She's deaf and cannot hear you talk. Go on, tap her now." She tapped on her shoulder with one hand and pointed at me with her other hand.

I suddenly saw one of the students in my peripheral vision talking to me. Mrs. Miller was great at cuing me about my environment. I decided to play along with Mrs. Miller and waited for the student to tap me on the shoulder. I wanted to help teach him about social etiquette — in other words, Deaf culture.

When Eli came up to me and started talking, I neither heard him nor saw him, but his peanut butter breath and puffs of air wafted by my face. He was a couple of inches away, but he did not tap my shoulder to get my attention. I laughed and turned to look at him.

"Please step back and try again. This time, tap my shoulder gently," I signed.

Being in a mainstreamed program without proper exposure to social skills, deaf children have a harder time learning the social norms of interacting with other deaf children, but it is still easier than it is with their hearing peers.

Wednesday, January 12

I was shocked to find out that the 'Science of Sounds' was going to be part of the curriculum. As Mrs. Feldman walked out of her classroom on the second floor, I marched over and quizzed her about the conflicting interest of teaching deaf students about the 'Science of Sounds'.

"Actually, Mr. Paynes wanted to empower the deaf students about their own hearing, and it gives them a greater understanding about their own hearing loss. It also helps the hearing students learn more about sounds and therefore, they can learn more about their deaf classmates." She explained.

I was dumbfounded. "Do you think it will invite opportunistic teasing?"

"No… the hearing students have been pretty good because they are aware that everybody is different, in a good way," she naively smiled.

Should I tell her about the time a hearing girl plucked Joey's CI off of his magnetized head? Or how about the two hearing boys who told Toby that the teacher had made an announcement that it was OK to kick the ball over the roof?

This type of teasing and manipulation happened all the time, and none of the teachers noticed.

As part of the socialization program, the deaf students in every grade level got to pick a couple of hearing classmates to play with during quiet time and field trips. Every year, Timmy chose the same two hearing girls, but they had started drifting away from him.

Most integrated programs have the same social progression. Kindergarten hearing students are unable to discern between deaf and hearing students. First grade hearing students have a vague idea that their deaf classmates are somewhat different, but the socialization aspect is still normal.

Second grade hearing students start to realize that there is something different about their deaf classmates. Toward the end of the school year, they start discriminating on the playground.

Third grade hearing students begin to understand clearly that their deaf classmates are different, they avoid their deaf classmates entirely by the time they enter the fourth grade.

By the fifth grade, total exclusion is practiced by the hearing classmates — even when there is a deaf kid that they actually like in the class. The deaf students are stuck playing with a limited number of other deaf students, whether they like each other or not.

Still standing in the hallway, I mentioned to Mrs. Feldman that Mrs. Jones told the deaf students to spell the words by sounding them out – solely as an ongoing supplement to the speech therapy and phonics sessions. It didn't make any sense to separate words and sounds into two things rather than to reinforce that they both mean the same thing.

"That is why the deaf students are in the mainstream deaf education program. The D/HH teachers are trained to deal with them."

Why did I bother? I smiled and went back to my tasks.

Later that afternoon, the deaf students were in Mr. Paynes' classroom for the science lessons. Alyssa started crying, so I quickly went to see what was wrong.

"I not know," she signed.

Cassie waved to get my attention.

I turned to look at her, and she signed in a defensive manner, "I asked Alyssa what vibration meant seven times!"

In confusion I asked, "Did Mr. Paynes ask the class what vibration meant seven times?"

"No, Alyssa did not say anything, so I asked her over and over because I didn't think she understood, or she wasn't paying attention to me. Each time I asked her what vibration meant, she just shrugged and said she did not know. I gave her the answer, and then I asked her the same question. Guess what? Alyssa still gave me that same dumb response over and over!"

I was shocked at Cassie's response because she was supposed to switch into the role of a teacher's aide whenever possible. She should already have experience with Alyssa's tendency to not answer questions.

"Oh, she needs a great deal of time to respond!" I replied. "If Mr. Paynes asked Alyssa something, then it makes sense to repeat it seven times. However, don't call her responses dumb," I cautioned.

I turned to Alyssa, and using signs simple enough for her to understand, I rephrased the question. "What causes vibration?"

Alyssa raised her head, looked up at me, and diminutively signed, "Energy."

Her answer was right, but by this time, Mr. Paynes' topic of discussion had progressed so far that Alyssa had fallen too far behind to catch up with the classroom discussion on the 'Science of Sounds.'

Tuesday, January 18

We walked into the music room, and the deaf children handed their microphones to the music teacher. She told the students to leave them on her desk.

I surveyed the room and wondered which the greater insult was: teaching deaf students the 'Science of Sounds', or teaching them the electric keyboards. I groaned, remembering the experience from last year.

After the music teacher demonstrated the keyboards and had the students practicing, Carmen became swamped, running back and forth across the room trying to demonstrate where the finger placements should be. Beads of sweat popped up on her forehead.

"Do you know how to use the piano?" She asked me.

Having observed the music teacher only helping the hearing students, I replied, "You are asking a profoundly deaf person if she knows how to play the piano. Ask the music teacher if you need help — it's her job to teach the deaf students where their fingers should be."

"The music teacher cannot service all of the deaf students at once. That's why I am helping her!" Carmen said defensively.

If the deaf students had been sitting in the same row, the Deaf row, it would have been much easier to help them without having to weave through the cramped desks, potentially knocking off the keyboards.

Alyssa was showing the most difficulty with using the electric keyboards. For the sake of her dignity, to prevent further embarrassment for the deaf students in the face of the hearing establishment, I walked over and offered my help, using basic ASL.

"See me not fingers," Alyssa signed and started to cry.

I tried to figure out what Alyssa meant by what she said, but from personal experience, I realized that Alyssa was having difficulty looking down at the keyboards on the electric piano and then looking back up at

117

the interpreter. By the time Alyssa looked back up, the teacher had already moved on.

It would have been easier if the music teacher had paused for Alyssa and Carmen to catch up, but she was unwilling to do that.

I explained to Alyssa, as I demonstrated, "Right here you have a sheet of song, 'Mary Had a Little Lamb', that has numerical sequences that tell you which fingers should be tapping on which keys."

Alyssa nodded elatedly and hugged me, smiling from ear to ear.

While I was working with Alyssa, Carmen walked over to Emma. She leaned over Emma's shoulders and started to manipulate Emma's fingers to show her the proper placement on the keys. I cringed. I knew Emma like the back of my hand. Emma hated excessive touching. I waved at Carmen to get her attention:

"Emma's fingers are stiff and she cannot bend them," I alerted Carmen.

"That's nonsense. She can learn to use all of her fingers. I used to be a physical therapist's assistant, you know," Carmen replied.

Emma became increasingly irritated at Carmen's excessive bending of her stiff fingers. Moving them across the keyboards caused her a great deal of discomfort. Feeling helpless, I tried to intervene, but Carmen would not listen.

Emma started to cry and pulled her hands away. Carmen grabbed them and placed them back on the keyboard. Emma tried to sign something, but Carmen would not let her hands go free. Emma's frustration built up to the point that she elbowed Carmen in the groin.

Carmen bent over clutching her groin and let out a loud "oomph!" The whole class stopped and looked at her. She regained her composure and said indignantly, "Did you see that?!"

Carmen began to scold Emma as the music teacher walked over to us and asked what was going on. I knew that it would be pointless to ask Carmen to interpret for me, so I began explaining to the music teacher in voice. Carmen quickly justified herself and dominated the conversation by talking over me.

118

Frustrated, I left the room and reported the incident to my boss, Mrs. Jones – she was in charge of me, because I monitored Emma for her. I also told her that the music teacher had left the microphones on her desk instead of wearing them around her neck while she walked around the room.

Mrs. Jones looked confused. "Didn't the music teacher show the deaf students where their fingers were supposed to be?"

I shook my head no. Mrs. Jones threw her hands in the air.

Thursday, January 20

After work, I went to a local gym to work out. Someone walked up behind me and tapped on my shoulder. I turned around and saw an old deaf acquaintance of mine. Saffiyah and I chatted a bit about my work, and as the conversation progressed, it dawned on me that she was a former student of Mrs. Jones'.

I could not believe it when she said that she was the one who had advised Jaber's parents to get the second CI when the first one failed. My knees buckled and I sat on the floor as I listened to her admit that she was also the one who encouraged them to send Jaber to an oral school out of state. By then, I was horrified.

"Didn't you realize that it would be a total failure for Jaber if he could not hear at all and was told to speak? The CI surgery destroyed all of the hearing in both of his ears!"

"He can feel his throat," Saffiyah quickly broke in.

This was ludicrous, because Jaber could not always touch other people's throats, in school for learning or later in life. It wasn't practical.

Thursday, January 27

Mrs. Miller, Cassie and I sat in the teacher's lounge discussing which deaf students should be in whose classrooms in the fall. Cassie said that Timmy would be in Mrs. Jones' room.

I was astounded.

"No way! Mrs. Jones' room is not stimulating enough for him!"

Cassie asked me to clarify what I meant.

119

"Timmy should not be in Mrs. Jones' room. Mr. Paynes has age appropriate sophisticated manipulatives, such as marble runs, puzzles and experimental pieces. He has a far more advanced environmental setting, while Mrs. Jones' free explorations only involve using calendars, cutting shapes for the corkboard and large manipulatives, like mega Legos, jumbo plastic vehicles and dominoes numbered from one to ten.

"Mrs. Jones' tools are even too simple for third graders. Emma and Toby's physiques are too tall to be socializing with kindergartners and one second grader. Don't get me wrong, Mrs. Jones is a decent teacher, but she specializes in teaching deaf students in kindergarten through second grade."

Mrs. Miller agreed with me.

"Well, if Timmy was in Mrs. Feldman's classroom, she would have a total of 10 deaf students. It is better to split them up and balance it out for the D/HH teachers." Cassie contended.

"At least Timmy will go to Mr. Paynes' class for the integration program this fall," I said, still concerned.

"No," Cassie corrected me, "Mr. Paynes complained to the principal that it was not fair for him to take the deaf students all the time. If the deaf child's parents have a problem with Mrs. Weaver, then let it be. If Mrs. Weaver continues to have problems with having deaf students in her classroom, then she should not be teaching at all." Cassie signed.

"Timmy is sensitive! Mrs. Weaver is too harsh and biased." I replied.

Cassie and Mrs. Miller both nodded and said that plans do sometimes change at the last minute.

I skipped recess duty to accompany Timmy, who hankered after me for a friend to talk with in ASL during his break. Mrs. Miller also stayed with me in the classroom, waiting for the kindergarten students to come in from recess.

From my peripheral vision, I noticed that a queue of deaf students passed by our door. I looked into the hallway to see whose class it was. Mrs. Smith and Brianne were accompanying the deaf pre-kindergartners.

Blossom waved at Mrs. Miller and me. As we waved back at her, Brianne quickly shoved Blossom's waving hand to her side and shooed her to quicken her pace.

Mrs. Miller signed behind a big book, so that Timmy would not see our private conversation.

"Did you see what Brianne just did?"

"Yes, I know. She isn't too crazy about you," I replied.

"But preventing a deaf girl from expressing her greetings to both of us is unacceptable from an interpreter," she said.

I nodded in agreement.

Later, when it was time for school to be out, Junie walked into the hallway.

Mrs. Smith stopped her and asked, "I heard there was supposed to be a bi-lingual and bi-cultural (bi-bi) charter school meeting tonight."

I walked past both of them. Junie slyly winked at me, and when she finished talking to Mrs. Smith, she caught up with me and asked, "Are you coming tonight?"

I nodded and quickly left.

That night at the bi-bi meeting, where concerned parents and deaf people gathered, I discussed replacing Mrs. Smith. That way, we could improve the relationship between the school and the parents of deaf students. We could provide a code of ethics workshop and offer sign language refresher courses to the interpreters. The people at the meeting were reluctant toward my idea, which was understandable. They were insistent on setting up a bi-bi charter school.

Friday, January 28

At the gym, the students were excited to be playing basketball again, especially the deaf students. Emma seemed to be okay with me leaving her if I stayed within a comfortable distance, so I found a place to sit and watched her mingle with the other students.

The gym teacher started to explain the rules of the game to the third graders. One of the deaf students started talking to the gym teacher, interrupting his instructions. Carmen interpreted the gym teacher's words to the student:

"Repeat spell meat... and don't interrupt me again."

I tried to figure out what the gym teacher could have meant, "Repeat spell meat." It didn't make any sense. Common sense told me that the gym teacher had said something meaningful, not what she translated. I waited until the game began for a good opportunity to ask her what she meant.

"I didn't sign that!" She said defensively.

I insisted that I'd seen it myself.

Carmen tilted her head backwards and signed, "Oh! Now I know what you are talking about. The gym teacher told the students to raise their hands if they want to speak up or ask questions."

Not wanting to inadvertently show her how it is done, I used my voice and asked her how to sign, "Raise your hand."

It still looked like, "Repeat spell meat."

Carmen saw that I proved my point and defensively minimized the situation:

"Looks a little alike, but it means the same, don't it," she said, smiling and walking toward Alyssa.

I cringed knowing what was about to happen. Carmen crowded Alyssa and pestered her. I returned to my spot and sat down watching as she continued to bump into Alyssa while Alyssa was trying to play the game. Carmen accidentally tripped Alyssa, knocking the ball out of her hands. It was one embarrassing blunder right after the next.

To the point of harassment, Carmen continued shouting out orders to Alyssa, "Move back! Less power! You shoot too hard! Do this with that foot...jump higher..."

I could not wait for gym class to be over. Watching Carmen do this to Alyssa was like what I imagine the screeching sound of nails on a chalkboard must be like for hearing people.

Tuesday, February 1

In reading the newspaper that morning, I saw an article that the bi-bi committee had written to the editor of the local newspaper. The article pointed out that Knight School did not have Deaf culture, had only two part-time deaf role models, had only one TDD or alert light signalers for the deaf, and had zero closed captioning programs. The list went on. However, the newspaper accidentally printed Junie's name instead of the 'Bi-Bi committee.' I wondered what consequences might come about in the future because of it.

The clock read 9:30, so I led the students into the cafeteria. I sat on a bench with the deaf students as we waited for Mr. Paynes' class to arrive for the violin lessons. Mr. Paynes then told the students to sit on the floor in three rows with ten students in each row, because there were only 10 violins.

Three of the deaf students, Alyssa, Brendan, and Toby, sat in the third row as they watched their classmates rehearse. I kept Emma with me behind the third row, where she would be less inclined to act inappropriately.

Kallie came in a little later and distracted the deaf students by doing a little hip-hop dance, waving both of her arms over her head. I asked her where Carmen was.

She sat next to Emma on my left, and she said that she was substituting for Carmen. Emma extended her left hand and gripped Kallie's right hand.

"If I were you, I wouldn't do that," I cautioned Kallie.

"Wh...Oh shit! Where have her hands been?!" Kallie exclaimed, trying to free her hand from Emma's tightened grip.

"You really don't want to know..." I replied, and I suggested that she go wash her hands.

As pale as a ghost, Kallie broke free and left. She returned a few minutes later.

This was Kallie's first time seeing the deaf students practice their violin lessons.

"Even in their fifth week of rehearsal, they sound horrible!" Kallie signed.

"Who sounds horrible?" I had no clue how the students performed.

"The deaf kids!" She replied. Her face frowned, and she pointed to the deaf students. "They look up at the instructor's finger placements and then look back down at their own. By the time they look up again, the teacher has moved far ahead."

I knew what she meant. I nodded aggressively and then reminded her that she should go up and interpret.

"But they just have to watch the violin instructor's hand movements. They're OK. They don't pay attention to me anyway."

A lump formed in my throat and it became difficult for me to swallow. That type of attitude did not belong here. If they only made occasional glances at the interpreter, then so be it. That was their ideal amount of maximum information, their own customized access. But the deaf students didn't have equal access because it was intentionally withheld from them, and they weren't even aware of it.

The deaf students looked adorable as they played their instruments, but as bad as Kallie said they sounded, it probably only fostered the hearing students' negative opinions of them. They then acted on those negative perceptions — cyclical stigma.

Perhaps it would have been better if there were separate lessons for the hearing and deaf peers, just for the sake of their dignity, especially during the music activities.

Kallie excitedly tapped on my shoulder to get my attention. She brought up a plausible solution. She suggested that the deaf students strain to pay attention to the pacing violin instructor, or that a music stand be set up to keep their music sheets in an upright position. Kallie also thought that color codes could be used on the neck of the violin to identify which string to pluck.

"Kinda too late for that now," I flatly pointed out. "Not only would the school budget not provide for such luxury accommodations, but there is only one week of violin lessons left."

The deaf students could not aurally recall the music notes on the strings, because some of their hearing aids and listening devices only worked half the time.

As the class was about to end, Kallie said that Joey's ability to sign had decreased greatly because he was the only deaf kid in Mrs. Weaver's class.

"What do you want me to do? Go up there and interpret?–please!" I said.

She slapped me on the arm and laughed.

"Ouch," I rubbed my arm.

The whole time that Kallie was sitting behind the three rows of students, she did not interpret or perform her required duties. She was busy talking to me. This was not a happy hour.

Later that day, Mrs. Smith stopped me in the hallway and asked if I thought that Blossom should be in Mrs. Jones' class in the fall. This was an awkward situation for me.

"I don't know how well prepared Blossom is for kindergarten," I replied.

Mrs. Smith raised her closed hand, extending her index and middle fingers, tapping them to her thumb (the sign for 'No') and said:

"No. What do you think of the article?" Apparently, she had read it as well.

I defended the article's views. "Junie felt that Blossom was not getting the language support that she needs at this school."

As soon as I started signing, Mrs. Smith disagreed with me. She should have let me finish my sentence before jumping to conclusions.

"It's wrong to force sign language on deaf children," she said.

I patiently waited for my turn. "Do any of the deaf children speak clearly?" I asked.

Without hesitation she defensively said, "Yes."

I immediately disagreed with her. "So, can people *other* than you, the families and the speech therapists understand the deaf child's speech?"

Mrs. Smith and I stared at each other quietly in a brief awkward pause.

"At some point in their lives, their speech will become clear," she claimed. "It takes patience and time. You know that's right; just look at you and your sister." Mrs. Smith then turned and walked off.

That is such a generalized myth. When one deaf person speaks well, it does not mean that all deaf children will grow up and speak well.

Wednesday, February 2

Somewhat guardedly, I walked into Mrs. Jones' classroom, not knowing how the D/HH teachers and interpreters would react to the bi-bi article.

Rhett's mom was waiting there to pick up her son from our classroom for a pre-kindergarten conference appointment. I looked around and waited for someone to say something.

"Did you see the letter to the editor in the newspaper yesterday?" She asked, mouthing the words.

I was afraid of this. I didn't know if she had used her voice or not, but I went ahead and nodded that I had. Out of the corner of my eye, I saw Mrs. Jones' hands fly in the air. She swiveled around in her computer chair and stormed toward her desk in the back of the room. I felt lousy because Junie's letter to the editor stirred some tension among the D/HH teachers and D/HH staff at school. The bi-bi committee only wanted a better education; who could blame them for that?

Rhett's mother withdrew from the room with her son, leaving me and Mrs. Jones in the room alone. I looked at the clock wishing that the students would arrive. I could not stand that awkward moment — deafening silence — knowing that she wanted to say something. My heart leapt into my throat when Mrs. Jones waved into my peripheral vision; I turned to look at her and apprehensively smiled.

"I sent you an email asking for your opinion about Junie's letter to the editor," Mrs. Jones signed, "but since you are here now, I will ask you in person. What do you think of this whole thing?" She made her way back across the room and sat on the padded swivel chair by the computer.

I took a deep breath and let it out slowly, trying to brainstorm about what I should say. Knowing that my job could be on the line, I decided to downplay the impact by clarifying vital information.

"First of all, the bi-bi committee sent that letter, and the newspaper printed Junie's name instead. The idea of having a bi-lingual and bi-cultural program here would not work because there are not enough deaf students and Deaf staff here to support the program," I signed, relinquishing the use of my deaf speech.

Was it me, or did I actually see her head nod and a smile? Thoughts ramped through my head.

Mrs. Jones replied, "Almost all of the deaf students here lack the skill and knowledge to use basic sign language. Now, Blossom is profoundly deaf. She deserves more sign language support, which is what we offer here."

I clenched my teeth as Mrs. Jones continued. My thoughts advanced to Alyssa, Joey, Timmy and other deaf students who lacked language support. They often went all day without an interpreter, especially in the special-related classes, such as gym, art and music.

Cassie and Carmen were notoriously late. I often had to leave Emma in the hands of her teachers to go and look for the tardy interpreters, only to find Cassie in the resource room chatting with a teacher, or Carmen panting as she made her way down the hall, appearing to have sneaked out to walk around the block for a cigarette break, because she reeked of cigarettes. Alyssa had to smell that, day in and day out.

Kallie was a chronic interrupter and distracter. I often found her at the computer or trailing idly behind the deaf students, creating distracting attention.

My focus trailed back to Mrs. Jones as she was saying, "Are we missing something that you think or feel we could offer more of?"

I was dumbstruck.

I remembered some time ago when I had brought up to the D/HH teachers and interpreters the lack of accessibility to Deaf culture, and they had ignored my concerns. I offered to volunteer to be the head interpreter, but it required the acceptance and approval of the D/HH teachers and interpreters. Most of the D/HH support staff would not accept a Deaf woman making responsible decisions and taking charge of their schedules. Except for Pamela, they had all denied my suggestions.

My thoughts returned to Mrs. Jones' continuing conversation.

"You know Paxton... His parents don't want him to use sign language," she said.

I interrupted, "I know about Paxton. I watched him do well without sign language. He's more orally proficient than most of the deaf students."

Per happenstance, Mrs. Smith walked into the room while Mrs. Jones was signing:

"You interrupted me and that was not my point. My point is that there are some parents who do not want their children to learn sign language at all. As for Paxton, his grandfather is blind, and the parents don't want him to be forced into using sign language. They are afraid that once he uses sign language, he wouldn't be able to communicate with his blind grandfather or vice versa. Do you understand? It is very unacceptable to force deaf students to use sign language if their parents are against it."

"But what about *tactile* sign language," I asked.

Mrs. Smith then interrupted into our private conversation and added, "Yes. I told Libby the same thing."

After dinner at my desk at home, I was having second thoughts about working at Knight, and I left the resignation letter unfinished.

Suddenly I had an epiphany. I shot a look at my roommate.

I heatedly signed, "I should ask Junie if the bi-bi committee has tried contacting the Deaf school to see if it is willing to notify the parents about the bi-bi school here! Perhaps the Deaf school could help establish a 'Regional Outreach Program' under the direct supervision and support of the Deaf school, instead of the AEA! What do you think?"

My friend nodded and signed, "Bring it up at the next bi-bi meeting!"

Monday, February 7

I took the deaf third graders to the gym and immediately groaned. The gym teacher had new lessons for Mr. Paynes' class. It was a gymnastics lesson. The students would be doing floor exercises as well as using a variety of gymnastics bars. That meant that I had to do all of the lifting and spotting. The gym teacher could not help me with Emma because he was busy helping the other students on the parallel bars. I shadowed Emma most of the time for her safety.

Carmen nagged Alyssa, "Take off your hearing aids! They flop out of your ears, and it makes you look silly."

Alyssa rubbed her hearing aid and spoke, "Fine is okay." After seeing Carmen's disapproving facial expression, Alyssa sighed and removed her hearing aid, then signed, "Is my fine."

All the other hearing aid wearers left the hearing aids in their ears.

The gym teacher called Alyssa up front to demonstrate her cartwheels and other floor exercises. Alyssa gleefully jumped up from her seat and ran over to the gym teacher. He told her what to do and she did it. While Alyssa was busy demonstrating her skills, Carmen came over to me.

"I did not interpret, and yet she understood the gym teacher! Without an interpreter! It's like Alyssa is really hearing and not deaf!"

When Alyssa was finished demonstrating her skills, the class clapped their hands. Carmen strolled over to Alyssa, who had a huge smile on her face as she tucked her shirt back down.

Alyssa screamed out, "I did it!"

"Nah, you need to point your toes some more," Carmen signed.

I tried to stop Carmen before she became too meddlesome, because Alyssa had performed better than most of the students in the class.

Carmen lashed out in one overbearing comment after another. Deciding this pettiness had to stop, I went over to Alyssa and applauded her for a spectacular performance. As predictable as she was, Alyssa hugged me.

More and more, I dreaded going into the teacher's lounge. It was becoming clear that they made sure it was not my world. Cassie tried her best to interpret several rapid-fire conversations the teachers were having at the same time.

Cassie signed, "Debate time! I want to put Deaf culture into the classroom setting."

"I'm opposed to forcing deaf students to learn to sign if the parents do not want them to learn. Let them be!" The resource room teacher declared.

Cassie slammed her fist down on the table and shot back forcefully, "How would you like it if you had deaf parents who taped your mouth shut to make you sign their language?"

The resource room teacher clammed up.

Mrs. Feldman jumped in, "At least we offer them language support."

Unexpectedly, I found that to be funny and my laughter threw them off guard. They stared at me with perplexity.

Cassie, as visibly stressed as I was, yelled and slammed the table. "Language support! Not incorporating Deaf culture and awareness equals ethnocide. Period." Cassie added this while she had the chance.

I got up and walked out of the teacher's lounge.

Hearing parents of Deaf children most often seem to want to train their kids to communicate with them – verbally, and hearing/listening; and so focus on teaching them *oralism* – to learn to make correct sounds aloud and to learn how to listen better – and they also seem to implicitly discount giving the kids any further instruction which would allow them to communicate with each other using sign language. This is one of the commonly seen characteristics of "audist" aversion.

Tuesday, February 8

It was 9:30 A.M., and Emma was getting antsy and pinch happy. She kept asking me whether her parents would show up to watch her play the violin. They lived over an hour away, and it was unlikely that they would show.

Mrs. Jones said to Emma, "Just do your best and show us what you've learned. Ask one of your favorite adults to sit and watch you play."

Knowing Emma, I stepped back out of her reach and watched her plot something. She was becoming fidgety, and it was time to go to the cafeteria and prepare the violin presentation for the guests.

Three rows of students assembled on the floor, while the violin teacher announced that each row of students would play the violins.

Emma sat on the bench with me and kept asking about her parents. When I told her that I did not know, she coughed in my face and began pinching me. I made her sit in front of me, slightly behind her peers, after she tried to hurt me.

The parents began trickling in, filling up the cafeteria. Emma waved at all of them and asked them in sign language, "You see my mom?"

I bent down from my bench to maintain level eye contact with Emma and quickly reminded her that none of them knew sign language.

"They know my mom!" She tried to make a convincing comeback.

Saddened by the fact that I had to explain this to her, I said, "They do not live one hour away like you do. If they did, their children would be going to the school where your brothers go."

As expected, Emma leaned over and tried to bite me on the leg.

The first row of students, all hearing, began their violin performances. Mrs. Jones entered in time to hear the second row of hearing students. Emma was becoming restless, and I reassured her that all of the adults would be proud of her.

By the time the second row of violinists ended their performances, Emma had broken her prescription eye glasses. Mrs. Jones told me to take her out of the cafeteria, because she would not be able to see the strings on her violin. Mrs. Jones was also concerned that Emma would hurt the other students in front of their parents and guests.

Oh well, so much for my effort. Emma could not help but feel disenchanted.

Wednesday, February 16

It was language development day, which happened every Wednesday from 9:30 to 10 A.M. in Mrs. Feldman's classroom. I found a spot with Kallie, Lauren and Cassie at the interpreter's desks in the back of the room. Mrs. Feldman was at the computer in the far corner of the classroom. The interpreters signed to each other about who would and would not be returning in the fall. Sidda would probably be going to her home district, they thought, leaving only Blossom, Rhett, and Kayla.

As Kallie continued to name names, Cassie interrupted, "I can hear the speech therapist forcing one of the students to pronounce the letter 'T' at the end of the word 'Bent.' He sounds like he is struggling to perfect the 'T' sound."

Kallie and I looked on as she paused. "The speech therapist just told him to try again, only to do *better* this time."

Cassie's eyes widened and she flailed her hands. "Oh my gosh! She should be in that deaf student's place, or at least hear herself from his perspective!" She signed sarcastically.

I quipped, "They're better off practicing their spelling words instead."

I looked over Cassie's left shoulder and watched the group of deaf students with their eyes fixed on the speech therapist. I felt sorry for them as they squirmed in their seats trying to produce the perfect 'T' sound.

"No, it isn't their fault. It's the parents! Know why?" Kallie was saying when I looked back.

We shook our heads no.

Kallie let loose her opinion. "Their parents do not know what their children are going through, because they don't see this happening. They are not clients or patients. The parents don't have to sit in this cramped little room. The parents want perfect speaking little deaf children so that they can belay their own sense of guilt, so that their children are 'as good as normal'. If the parents objected to this psychological torture, this ridiculous arrangement would not be approved in the first place. I think they should use sign language. A lot of their children's speech sucks, and isn't clear enough to be used publicly anyway."

Cassie and Lauren covered their mouths trying to suppress an outburst of laughter as the speech therapist continued teaching the deaf students how to pronounce irregular verbs.

It is not entirely the parents' fault. It is the Audiologists, the Speech Pathologists, Ear Nose and Throat Specialists, and the policy makers' faults as well ... the audist professionals in general are milking deaf children for medical funding. Most deaf children are *healthy*!

The experts' motto must be: "There's No Money In Solutions!"

Every Wednesday, for 30 minutes, this practice of pronouncing irregular verbs and all other kinds of exercises was considered an essential part of their learning. They had been in speech programs since pre-kindergarten, and most of them still could not speak well. Most of them would never even catch up to their peers.

That afternoon, Carmen and Lauren were both gone, which meant that the fourth and fifth graders did not have an interpreter. Cassie translated for the third graders in the special-related class, but six of the deaf students went through the day without learning because they were without interpreter service.

During the last period, Kallie waltzed into Mr. Paynes' classroom and teasingly danced toward me, mischievously jabbing my arm. I tried to avoid jabbing back because all of the students were staring at us — at Kallie's distracting performance.

Cassie looked perturbed at Kallie. I watched Mr. Paynes as he ground his jaws and tried to regain control of his students' attention. From 30 feet away, Cassie waved at me to get Kallie's attention. I told Kallie to look at Cassie.

"Did you know that the fourth graders have no interpreter right now?" Cassie asked.

"Yeah, so?" Kallie replied.

"Get your butt over there and interpret for them!" Cassie muted her voice and laughed.

The class was making Valentine cards. I was immersed with helping Emma handle the scissors, until I turned and looked at Cassie. She was fussing at Alyssa for not following directions.

She explained to Alyssa, "I signed in the air for nothing. If you had been listening to the directions, you would not have screwed up your Valentine card."

I thought Cassie's comment was uncalled for. Alyssa's card actually looked pretty good. A couple of the hearing classmates went wild with their cards, and Mr. Paynes had liked them.

As soon as I returned my attention to Emma, I noticed that she had cut off a whole lock of hair from her forehead. She now looked like she had a receding hairline. Oops.

Friday, February 18

Every Friday, Knight employees brought breakfast into the library. As I was piling food on my plate, I noticed the secretary make a profane ASL sign to the librarian. The secretary caught me staring at her and laughingly told Mrs. Feldman to look at me. Mrs. Feldman turned and saw me staring at the group in disgust.

Mrs. Feldman tried to excuse them. "I taught them that because they wanted to know a sarcastic sign for…"

I broke my eye contact with hers and walked away with my plate of food.

The secretary yelled at Donna to get my attention. Donna tapped me on the shoulder and told me to look at the secretary. The secretary looked at me, stuck her tongue out sideways and signed, "Time sheet."

"I know it's due today. I'll give it to you today. Be patient," I told her as I gestured, "Relax."

Later that afternoon, Timmy had indoor recess due to his asthmatic condition. He chose to play in our classroom alone rather than with the 24 hearing students in Mrs. Rickham's class. As usual, Mrs. Jones left him under my supervision during my lunch break. I didn't complain because of the pitiful adversity that fell upon the deaf students. I wanted to rectify the situation whenever I could.

I sat by the computer and asked Timmy why he chose to play alone.

He corrected me, "Best talk with you. You more fun talk. You busy?"

I logged off the computer and turned to look at Timmy as he crept toward me. He kept one hand on his head above his ear and asked me what he had in his hand. I told him I had no idea. He begged me to guess.

"Your CI?" I said.

He giggled and signed, "Nope," with his left hand, keeping his right hand to his head careful to conceal the secret item he was holding.

"You ready? You want know?" He signed.

I begged him to reveal the mystery.

Timmy slowly took his right hand off of his head.

I gasped and didn't know whether to laugh or to cry, but Timmy's rotund belly shook from laughing. He had made himself such a silly sight. He had a magnetized ball on his magnetized head. The ball jiggled as he laughed. That made our day. That certainly made up for the loss of his friend, Mike.

One hundred percent seclusion is not socially healthy for students like Timmy. Hearing schools think they are doing a noble service for the deaf students, when in reality, they are doing it for themselves and the parents. It is better for the deaf students if there is more than one deaf child in a self-contained classroom; the more the better.

Cassie was on her way to the library when we bumped into each other. I told her about Mrs. Feldman having taught the Knight staff inappropriate signs. Cassie's face turned red and she clenched her fists.

"Very unprofessional of Mrs. Feldman to do that. I expected better from her. I see the staff using the B-word, the F-word and the A-word all the time as they pass each other in the hallway. They think it's cute and silly... Carmen, however, is the worst. Did you know that she is teaching SEE 2 at the district school board at nights? They each pay Carmen $40 every four weeks for her lessons! They should not pay her that much."

That meant that everyone at the school board was learning incorrect sign language from this woman. I shuddered at the thought. Carmen's signed words and the generic signed words did not have the same definitions.

As I walked toward Mrs. Jones' class, Brianne pulled me aside. She justified why Junie did not think that she interpreted. She said that she felt no need to when Mrs. Miller held the book and signed at the same time. I chuckled to myself at these excuses; Brianne would not even look Mrs. Miller in the eye or be near her.

As far as Blossom's father, Brianne reminded me about the confrontation with the principal concerning the lack of language support for Blossom. She said that Blossom's father had walked in while Mrs. Miller had one half of the group and she had the other half, and that he had misunderstood the entire situation and had jumped to conclusions. I suppressed my opinion about her two-faced lie.

This mainstream deaf education was an education, but it could hardly be called exceptional while it lacked adequate support services. Often, it seemed everyone cared more about their jobs than about the students.

Friday, March 4

Katy, a student interpreter, had been at the school for over a week for her internship. Katy and Blossom's mother Junie were friends and classmates. She sometimes went to Blossom's house to babysit Blossom. This existing friendship had an impact on Mrs. Smith.

That morning, Blossom walked into our classroom and sat down with Katy at the table. They began to play with cardboard puzzles. Minutes later, Mrs. Smith stormed into the room and yelled at Blossom for leaving the pre-kindergarten classroom without letting her know of her whereabouts. Everyone in the room was shaken by this outburst. Blossom knew where Katy was, and she wanted to see her.

That afternoon in the art classroom, Katy discussed the matter with Cassie. I told Katy that it was not her fault, and that she should not feel lousy.

Cassie jumped in, "Don't let Mrs. Smith make you feel this way. You're not the first one, nor will you be the last."

Katy cocked her eyebrows.

The situation certainly could have been handled better. Mrs. Smith could have patiently explained to Blossom why it was important to not simply wander off. "Let us know when you leave the classroom. Next time, do not wander off by yourself." She could then finish off with a smile. Deaf students, and all students, need to feel secure.

Cassie elbowed me and Katy to do something about it — like tell the principal or call her parents. I reminded Cassie that they probably would listen to her better.

"Really? Why?" Cassie skeptically asked.

"Because you're hearing, Cassie!" I replied.

Later that afternoon, the lady (I never got her name) who had been substituting for interpreter Brianne in Mrs. Smith's class, walked into our classroom and apologized for allowing the situation to get that far out of control. She thought it was an alternate day, because Blossom wanted to go to Mrs. Jones' room. She had allowed Blossom to go. The substitute held her hand in front of her mouth, trying to stop herself from crying.

Oddly enough, this woman who was substituting for Interpreter Brianne did not know sign language.

"Mrs. Smith just screams and screams at the students. I had to be in there to work with her and hear it. These children are only 3, 4 and 5 years old!" She continued to cry.

We immediately comforted her with our experiences with Mrs. Smith. Cassie said that she would call Junie about it that night. I, too, agreed to email her.

Then it occurred to me: the school is supposed to have a list of back-up interpreters on call. Why did they hire someone who did not know sign language? Surely that violated many mandated procedures.

Wednesday, March 9

Cassie met me in the school lobby. She informed me that Junie had called her and started crying on the phone.

Cassie wiped a tear from her eye and finished her sentence, "Junie said that when she put Blossom down for bed, Blossom had signed meekly, 'Me scared Smith'."

After hearing that, it was no wonder why I hadn't seen Blossom. Junie had immediately withdrawn Blossom from Mrs. Smith's class, literally yanking her out.

Cassie and I spotted Mrs. Smith walking around sullenly. She had puffy red eyes and a red nose, and she had obviously been crying.

The principal came up to Cassie and me in the hallway. He asked Cassie to interpret.

"Did you know that I am investigating the screaming incident? Were you in the room?"

I nodded.

"Keep this to yourself," he said and then left.

"I gotta go to work," Cassie said. "Meet me at recess when you pick up Emma. There is something else we need to talk about."

Later, as I walked past room 112, I noticed Mrs. Smith and Brianne's rapidly moving mouths and reddened necks, which seemed to indicate that they were arguing loudly.

When I went outside to retrieve Emma from her recess, Cassie asked to speak with me privately. She went on to vent her frustrations about the secretary wanting the Knight staff to get together and create several obscene signs in front of the camera for the principal's retirement party.

Cassie said that she told the secretary, "This truly insults my profession! To ask someone to teach all the others how to sign bad words is just debasing my career. What if the principal took it the wrong way and potentially has me fired? Have you thought about the consequences? I would prefer the staff use humorous signs, like pose as the Warrior mascot or something."

"Notice they asked you instead of me," I replied in disgust. "Don't you find that odd? It would be like me asking another deaf person how to pronounce a certain word, instead of asking a hearing person."

"They probably thought you would be offended. What other reason would they have for not asking you?" Cassie said.

I digressed and told her about how I was being treated by the secretary:

"She always asks the other employees to remind them about the time sheets," I signed. "If I happen to be in the office, she walks up and harshly signs right in my face, 'Time sheet'. Then she laughs in a sarcastic manner.

"I kept trying to explain to the secretary that harsh movements scream sarcasm and insult."

Cassie nodded and agreed with me, "The secretary is taking the sign language classes that Carmen is teaching at the school board. Imagine that! The secretary learned this sign movement from her."

The more I talked about it, the more furious I became with Carmen's code of ethics. It is inappropriate for the employees to be selectively biased and to learn only certain R-rated signs for their own benefit.

The day continued to hold surprises. Mrs. Feldman was scheduled to go on maternity leave soon. She asked the principal to hire Mrs. Miller as a substitute teacher. The principal questioned Mrs. Feldman about Mrs. Miller's capabilities as a deaf teacher and whether she could understand the deaf students. Mrs. Feldman affirmed that Mrs. Miller was capable of doing the job. Mrs. Miller had been substituting at Knight for a number of years by now — and the principal still felt the need to *question* her abilities?

Monday, March 14

Mrs. Miller was now in Mrs. Feldman's class until she returned from her maternity leave. One of the students with an interesting situation was Allen. Allen's mother wanted him to go to his home school district, so that he could behave like a normal hearing kid without an interpreter. She wanted Allen to be normal. She laid a guilt trip on the boy, causing him to sink into a state of depression. She wanted Allen to know that he had imperfect hearing and what an inconvenience that was to her. He was unable to meet her expectations. Allen saw that he was imperfect in his mother's eyes, and therefore, he strove to be something that he was not.

His mom told him that he would have a note taker, which created a problem because the school could not pay for a personal assistant due to budget limitations. D/HH inclusive programs are only available at a limited number of schools.

I asked Mrs. Miller who the note taker would be.

"It turns out that it is a classmate! Imagine that! A student cannot be expected to write fast enough or on a professional level! Allen is bound to run into problems." Mrs. Miller replied.

Changing the topic, I asked Mrs. Miller if she planned to go to the Roundup FunVenture the next day. She said that she did.

That night, Junie emailed to inform me that the principal had consulted with the head of the Special Education Department, and they came to the conclusion that no aberrant behavior had taken place between Mrs. Smith and Blossom.

"The principal told me that he and the head of the Special Education Department have been best buddies since Vietnam, and to top it off, they're golfing buddies as well. They aren't going to do anything about Mrs. Smith because the principal trusts the Special Ed head's judgment, and that is wrong!"

Impropriety indeed…

Tuesday, March 15

It was 9:15 in the morning and the deaf students were excited about going to the Roundup FunVenture. All of them had arrived and been accounted for except Timmy. Two of the D/HH teachers, their room interpreters and the deaf students met in the school lobby before getting on the school bus. Mrs. Smith and her class lingered behind.

At the event, it was the same ritual dance. All the special education children lined up with all the deaf students at the Roundup booths to make crafts, eat snacks, dance and listen to the music.

Mrs. Miller, Cassie and I all stood together observing the deaf students, then Kallie wedged her way into our group. A few exchanges of casual conversation ping-ponged back and forth, when suddenly, Kallie began to gyrate her butt against my thigh — apparently to the rhythm of the music. I gasped.

As my thigh was being polished, in embarrassment, I shoved the thigh-polisher away.

There were eyes all around. Several of the children and adults saw the butt rubbing incident. I thought I was going to die right on the spot. I found a way out by using Emma as an excuse. I quickly ushered her to another booth. Just as I was about to make my escape, I felt a painful slap on my butt.

I turned to see Kallie's arm retreating to her side. She had a big grin on her face. I kept on scooting Emma away from her. Kallie's butt slapping tendencies were terribly embarrassing and painful.

Mrs. Miller followed me across the room and asked, "What was that all about?"

"She always does that to me in front of everyone else. Mrs. Feldman even thinks it's funny," I shrugged.

"But there are kids around!" She said, covering her eyes.

Cassie saw our conversation and jumped in, "I just push her aside or slap her back. She doesn't care what you do as long as she succeeds in embarrassing you."

Mrs. Miller gasped in horror.

Sometimes part of audism is where hearing people feel guilty for enjoying music in front of Deaf people, so they then project the pain of that guilt outward, blaming the Deaf for not being able to participate in their enjoyments, and also for somehow deliberately depriving them of it just by existing.

After the final farewell band at 11:30, we went back to the school. I immediately disappeared into the art room for my lunch. This was the perfect hiding place. It was located in the basement and tucked away from the main hallway and foot traffic. There was silence. I saw no one for half an hour.

Mrs. Miller popped her head into the room.

"What are you doing in there?!" she asked.

"Come in. Lunch." I motioned to my food.

"Do you know the AEA itinerant audiologist?"

I shrugged, trying to picture a face.

"The obese one with stringy flat brown hair," she described, making a gesture of a fat waistline.

I shoved the last piece of food in my mouth and signed, "Yes. I've seen her around."

Mrs. Miller stepped into the classroom and I informed her that I only had about 20 minutes left.

"Since Mrs. Feldman is gone to have her baby, I have a problem with the itinerant audiologist. She refuses to speak directly to me. She prefers to speak to the interpreters about students' stuff."

Mrs. Miller paused and flicked her hands in the air. "She should address me directly about the students' hearing aids, trainers and microphones, because I am the one who reports problems and newly arisen issues to Mrs. Feldman, you know?"

With one hand I signed, "It's like she's insulting you. I have always felt that she didn't like my presence around the deaf students. She consistently refuses to acknowledge my presence."

"Exactly!" Mrs. Miller nodded and said, "Tell me what you have experienced or why you have felt this way. Perhaps our experiences are different?"

"Well, there are a few possible reasons here. I think it's because I don't wear hearing aids, and I kind of hinted to her that hearing aids are a waste of time. The students have to leave their table to give their hearing aids to the audiologist for her to inspect. Then, she calls the deaf students back one-by-one to return them. Then, they have to put it on, perform a sound check and return to the table to resume their learning environment. Too much back and forth going on. Lots of educational information gets lost in the process."

"Right!" Mrs. Miller nodded in agreement. "She comes at the least opportune times—during naps, during tests, and she even embarrasses them by calling them out of the hearing classrooms!"

After my break, I walked into Mrs. Jones' classroom and saw the AEA speech therapist talking with Mrs. Jones. After they finished discussing the deaf students' speech schedule, Mrs. Jones told me that they wanted Blossom to stay in Mrs. Smith's classroom. If Blossom ended up being here, Mrs. Smith would only have a couple of deaf students this fall.

Not long after, a woman from a neighboring school district came in and spoke with Mrs. Jones. She needed more support in convincing the hearing parents of a deaf girl that SEE was more advantageous than ASL. I knew the hearing parents; the mother was the director of the ASL Interpreter Training Program at a local community college.

After the woman left, I asked Mrs. Jones if the mother of the deaf girl knew that this meeting was taking place. Mrs. Jones shook her head no.

That evening, I emailed the interpreter training program director to let her know about this impromptu meeting.

Thursday, March 31

After spring break, Mrs. Miller continued to substitute for Mrs. Feldman. Blossom returned to Knight and became a new student in Mrs. Jones' class! It was Eli all over again, and we all had our hands full.

Friday, April 1

It was a new month, and the end of a week. All the flowers around Knight School started blooming heavenly aromas. I got a kick out of having office space with windows next to the flowering trees.

Typically on Fridays, the gym and music teachers combined two of the third grade classes outside on the playground. I spotted Lauren interpreting for the deaf students. After the teachers were finished explaining about the use of free time, I asked Lauren why she was here instead of Carmen. Lauren explained that early in the year the principal wanted to rotate the third through fifth grade interpreters, but he had not updated the rotation schedules for quite some time.

Lauren, the gym and the music teachers stood together near the entrance rather than be among the students. The special-related teachers chatted with Lauren. She listened with intent and signed in ASL, "That's awful."

"What's up?" I asked Lauren.

Lauren explained that the special-related teachers' hours had been cut and that they would be working for two different schools this fall.

"Too bad," I thought. "I will definitely miss the art teacher."

I got immensely jaded watching the three staff moving their mouths at rapid speed, so I strolled over to where many of the students were playing.

From the corner of my eye, I saw Lauren follow behind me and join the students playing kick ball. I had trouble following the kickball game because everyone spoke from several directions, so I retreated to a different play area where some of the students were playing four squares. From then on, Lauren and I monitored the playground while the gym and music teachers stayed near the school's back entrance.

Several of the deaf students saw me watching the hearing students play the four squares game and immediately ran to get in the queue to play. One by one, the hearing students lost until it was Toby's turn to get into the first square.

After a few minutes of playing, three of the hearing students told Toby that he was out of the game because he had bounced the ball too high.

Brendan joined the game. The same three students told Brendan that he was out of the game because he bounced the ball with both hands.

"Hmmm, that's odd," I thought. "The hearing students did the exact same thing and did not get eliminated from the game."

I watched more closely. Alyssa was the third deaf student to play. Just as I expected, the three hearing students told Alyssa that she was out of the game because the ball touched the line. My eyes told me otherwise.

To my horror, the hearing students were systematically targeting the deaf students, their own peers. I reported this matter to the special-related teachers, but they disregarded my concerns.

I took over the game and told the hearing students that I would be the referee. After I stopped talking, they made faces, groaned and shooed at me.

Quickly I reviewed the rules for the deaf students in ASL. They understood me, and the game began again. One-by-one, the hearing students were replaced with different hearing students. Starting with a clean slate, I thought that the new set of hearing students would not be as biased as the previous ones.

Boy was I wrong!

I had to take over and referee the game. The deaf students were unbelievably thrilled. Apparently, they had been hoping for someone to stand up for them.

At 10:05, one of the special related teachers blew the whistle to end the free time. The homeroom teachers gathered their students into their own queues. I filed in with Emma and Toby behind Mr. Paynes. Lauren grabbed Joey out of Mrs. Weaver's queue and took him with us because he typically forgot that he had one-on-one reading time with Mrs. Jones.

Mrs. Jones, however, always left the reading responsibility up to Lauren. The IEP specifically stated that Mrs. Jones was to read with Joey. That did not happen.

At the table, I watched Mrs. Jones review some assignments with Emma and Toby. Since Emma's behavior was manageable, Mrs. Jones told me to take a break. I went to the interpreter's desk and sat down.

I quietly observed Lauren and Joey. They sat on the floor where we have the community circle in the mornings.

Lauren signed a story about dolphins to Joey. Part of the story was about beached dolphins. I was horrified by the way Lauren signed the SEE 2 words 'washed up' to Joey. He did not understand the concept of 'washed up'. Lauren was becoming more and more frustrated as she tried to explain what it meant by using the same incorrect words, over and over.

She kept signing the word 'washed' by using the definition of 'rubbing together,' as if someone were washing their hands in the sink. She ended the word with 'up' by pointing in a skyward direction. Washed up dolphins do not mean 'hands washing in the sink and ending up way in the sky'.

I quickly rose from my seat and trotted over to Joey. I excused myself for intruding into their reading session, and seized Joey's attention. I signed the words 'washed up' in one simple ASL sign, using both hands. I used my left forearm as the beach and my right hand to sign the dolphins being stuck on the beach.

Joey's face lit up.

"Oh! You mean the dolphins became stuck on the beach?" He mimicked my signs of washed up dolphins.

I smiled and nodded yes.

Lauren craned her neck, looked up at me and smugly grinned.

146

ASL is a natural language, I thought to myself. How hard is it to understand, or for *them* to accept this fact?

Friday, April 15

I had noticed Joey sitting alone by the fence during the last recess, since the beginning of the week. I strolled over and asked him why he had time out.

In perfect SEE 2, he signed that he kept forgetting to give Mrs. Weaver the assigned microphone.

> "I forgot to give Mrs. Weaver the microphone in the morning when I came in her class on Monday. Then I forgot to hand the microphone back after recess on Tuesday, and then I forgot..."

> I interrupted him and used my ASL, "Every day you forgot?"

> "Yes," said Joey without signing.

It seemed ridiculous to me to entrust such young children with such expensive equipment. Mrs. Weaver could have easily walked a few steps to the microphone to get it herself, but it dawned to me that Joey might be her F-L-K.

When he got out of time-out, Joey had trouble keeping up with the jump rope games. His CI kept falling off every time his feet hit the ground. Several of the hearing students snickered after the CI fell onto the blacktop. Joey looked like he wanted to continue, but the CI was in the way, so I discreetly rushed to him and offered to hold his CI out of sight. Joey looked left and right and declined my offer, so I retreated.

At the four squares game, just as I expected, the hearing students were cheating against the deaf students again. It did not surprise me when the deaf students gave up and moved on to other, more lonesome, isolated activities such as playing with the hula-hoop, bouncing the ball against the wall and jumping rope.

The deaf students rarely played together. They wanted to do different things. They were embarrassed to be seen with each other around the hearing students. Their behaviors were entirely different inside the classroom. They associated more. Out in public, they tended to avoid each other.

At home on the sofa, I thought about the four squares game. This is what happened, in my early years at the Deaf school, when I was just about 11 years old. The Deaf students with Deaf parents would dominate the four squares.

Any deaf kid with hearing parents who tried to join would be systematically targeted, just as I had seen today. My Deaf peers systematically targeted the newcomers that came from hearing families or, as we called them, 'lousy signers', and the ones that spoke impeccably, 'hearie'.

In the inclusive setting, the orally skilled deaf students acted superior to the mute deaf students. This social behavior was totally opposite at the Deaf school, because a lot of times, the Deaf kids with Deaf parents thought they were superior to the orally proficient deaf kids and the deaf kids with hearing parents.

Another social aspect I observed was that the Deaf students at Deaf school thought that the deafer they were, the better they were. The deaf students at the hearing schools thought the more they could hear, the better they were.

I thought about when the BTE hearing aids were introduced with four different settings. One was the lowest setting, usually for the hard of hearing students. The profoundly deaf students usually go all the way to four.

As a mainstreamed young girl in the late 70's, I wore my hearing aids with the volume set on four. Most of my deaf classmates had the volume set on one. My classmates with the volume set on one would tell me that they could 'hear' and make fun of my profound deafness. That changed in the early 80's when my parents enrolled me in a Deaf school. I met many Deaf students, and the majority of them did not wear hearing aids at all. Some of them made fun of me for being 'hearing-like'.

They clearly labeled me right from the start, "You wear hearing aids! You hearie!"

At the Deaf schools, they were not ashamed of being profoundly deaf or for choosing not to wear hearing aids. They were proud of their identity. The Knight inclusive deaf students lacked that inner gem.

Thursday, May 5

Emma gave the music teacher the microphone. The music teacher tucked it in her back pocket rather than hang it around her neck. She was supposed to speak directly into the microphone. The deaf students could not hear her at all with it so far away from her mouth.

Emma and I sat near each other within arm's reach. The music teacher became incensed when I refused to sit on the carpeted area with everyone else. I felt fine sitting on the hard linoleum floor. All the students moved onto the carpeted area — except Emma and me. There was a reason for this. Emma needed to be away from the other students in case she decided to act up; in those cases, there was no telling what she would do. The music teacher glared at us.

As she talked about the new lesson, she methodically walked towards me and stopped in between me and Emma. Then she continued to walk around the room. A sickening odor assaulted my nostrils, and I immediately looked at Emma, who was already giggling. I asked her if she passed gas and, covering her face, she replied that she had not. She pointed to the music teacher who was already at the other end of the room.

"What do you mean it was her? How do you know that?" I asked.

"I heard her fart on the microphone," she spoke, rather than signing.

Emma stuck out her tongue and made a raspberry sound and laughed again.

I looked at the pocket on the music teacher's shorts, and sure enough, there was the microphone. The microphone had transmitted the farting sound to all of the deaf students' hearing aids.

Near the end of the lesson, she did exactly the same thing on her way back. She paused right in front of me, before moving on to her chair.

She farted in my face, and Emma heard it from the microphone.

Emma giggled and signed, "Bad teacher bad."

Friday, May 13

That morning, Mrs. Jones had the deaf students sit in a community circle, and taking turns, each child shared some news.

After the news, Mrs. Jones explained that she would be teaching new things about all kinds of food. She informed them that they would be eating a different type of food every day in order to learn about healthy foods.

Just as she signed the word 'eat' with a closed fist and thumb on the lip, similar to the manual letter 'A', Blossom jumped up from sitting on her bottom and landed on Mrs. Jones' lap. She started to criticize Mrs. Jones' sign for the word 'eat'.

"No! That's 'nut'! You wrong! You must sign that way 'eat', not 'nut'." She continued to demonstrate the ASL signed word for 'eat' (using the very similar ASL word for 'food').

Mrs. Jones reflexively put up her arm against Blossom's chest and told her to go sit back down. She collected herself from the innocent, but mistaken, criticism and looked at me. She said that the signed words for 'eat' and 'food' in ASL are alike, trying to justify herself for being pro-SEE 2 over ASL.

"Hmm," I thought to myself. Blossom wasn't talking about 'food'; she was talking about 'nut'. These words have different hand movements. But, Mrs. Jones had a point. A lot of ASL words do have similar signs with different meanings. SEE 2, if done properly, still has its own problems. But the biggest problem is that ASL is used in Deaf culture and SEE 2 is used in inclusive school programs and in many interpreter training programs.

It got me thinking about the young deaf students in the inclusive programs in public schools who do not have rich vocabulary skills because of their lack of exposure to a visual language. In reality, teachers should sign in ASL — the language most fitting the deaf and most used by the Deaf.

Deaf children from Deaf parents have rich language exposure, equal to hearing children of either hearing or deaf parents. However, deaf children from hearing parents usually have limited language exposure; very limited, because, sadly, most of the parents and siblings do not sign

150

or communicate thoroughly with the deaf child. These are most often the students put into inclusive programs.

The young mainstreamed deaf students with CI need more exposure to expand their vocabularies. One has to sign specific signs for each word to teach vocabulary, especially from kindergarten through second grade. To complicate matters, deaf kindergartners through second graders are, as they were at Knight, lumped into one class — often with children whose disabilities far exceed that of simply being deaf. Third, fourth and fifth graders are also lumped together in one classroom.

It is confusing for the children, because one interpreter signs a word differently from their parents or their D/HH teacher, using a completely different sign for the same word. Different signs for the same word confuse the deaf child, much the same as it would confuse a hearing kindergartener to have to learn all the different forms of a simple word such as 'dog' in English, Chinese, Hebrew, Latin, Arabic, French, Spanish, Polish, German and Italian — simultaneously. Multiply that by every word in the young child's already limited comprehension of vocabulary, and such complexity delays the child's linguistic opportunities until about the third grade.

When I signed ASL to the young kindergarten through second grade students, they had no idea what I was talking about. When I signed ASL to the third through fifth graders, they understood immediately. However, when I signed specific words in ASL grammar, using facial and body expressions, they still understood me. Therefore, it comes down to using specific words, such as 'gray' and 'eat', with consistency.

Monday, May 16

The school planned a fund-raising party during a minor league's baseball game. An interpreter service from Knight was provided for this event. All of the students had to buy a ticket if they wanted to go. All of the deaf students, except Timmy, bought tickets. The students excitedly talked about meeting each other at the game and about the food that would be there. Timmy felt left out. Mrs. Jones asked him if he wanted to go to the game. His face lit up and he nodded excitedly.

Mrs. Jones went to the library and spoke to the librarian. Together, they purchased three tickets — one for Timmy, one for his younger brother and one for his mother.

When the game night came, the moderator of the event drew a name from a box and Timmy's name was picked. The news cameras scanned the audience for Timmy, but there was no sign of him anywhere. It became apparent that Timmy never showed up for the game.

The following Monday, we asked Timmy why he could not come.

He mutely signed, "Car broke."

We knew that Timmy's stepfather worked weekend night shift, Thursday through Tuesday.

"How did your stepfather get to work?" Donna questioned Timmy.

Timmy looked at all the other deaf students to make sure that they weren't watching him and he quickly signed, "He drove."

Donna patted Timmy on the back and walked toward me. She reduced her spatial signing to conceal her hands from the view of the students:

"How do you explain that? Car broke? My ass!" She clutched her fist and scowled. "Damn mother!"

During my lunch break in the classroom, Donna, Mrs. Jones and I sat around one of the tables. I lip-read Mrs. Jones' comment, "I paid for Timmy out of my own pocket. The librarian dipped into the library funds to pay for the other two. $15 wasted."

I asked Mrs. Jones if the mother knew beforehand that the tickets were paid for. She said yes, and that she had even offered to drive them to the game.

Donna shook her head and signed, "I don't understand how his mother can do this to him, all of those empty promises she makes. How can she do this? Almost all happy events, he isn't there, like the Roundup FunVenture."

We stopped talking when Timmy ran into the classroom from recess.

I left the others and went to the playground to search for Emma. When I found her, she was mercilessly picking on Alyssa. I stepped in to rescue her.

I thought about how some of the teachers did not discipline the deaf students for turning in their homework late, or even at all. I remembered the librarian told the students to write a page about their hero. It took the deaf students several months to type two paragraphs, while it only took the hearing students two weeks to turn in one full page. It was understandable that they got behind, but the teachers should have given them incentives to motivate them. The biggest incentive to get the deaf students to do their homework would be to require the parents to sign it.

That night we had our fourth bi-bi charter meeting at a local community college. The number of supporters dwindled, probably because most of them knew that setting up the bi-bi charter school would not be successful unless we had more deaf students with deaf parents. Reality set in. I tried to get them to see that my idea of an "Outreach Program," where the Deaf school could share or provide external support to selected inclusive programs would probably work.

Lisa, the mother of Deaf twin sons, cautioned that the Deaf school threatened litigation against the bi-bi charter committee, because supporters were trying to convince the legislators to cut the interpreting program from public schools.

The Deaf school superintendent said that the basis of their argument for cutting the interpreting programs with low numbers of deaf students was to save the state money — after all, why did we have Deaf school? Closing the small interpreting programs would force the sign language dependent students to go to the Deaf school. This had proven to be successful in another state.

I interjected, "This might be a good opportunity to start a petition drive to get rid of Mrs. Smith, because otherwise she has ironclad teacher's union membership."

Lisa waited until I finished before she presented her potentially troubling point. "The AEA itinerant teacher for the deaf has refused to sign papers that allow or authorize my sons to transfer to the Deaf school. She hasn't returned my phone calls or emails. I don't know what to do. If the bi-bi charter goal isn't progressing, then the Deaf school is where I want to send my boys."

Shocked at the AEA caseworker's unprofessionalism, I asked Lisa if she had moved on to higher authority.

"Yes. What's even worse," she said, "is that she refuses to sign over my sons because her brother went to the Deaf school. He didn't come out the same person. She didn't want my sons to end up like her brother, always stuck at the Deaf school, avoiding his hearing family."

I listened intently as she continued to explain, "The AEA teacher's deaf brother chose to adopt the Deaf community as part of his life and identity, which took precedence in his daily affairs and which meant less time with his hearing family. That is the same path that she thinks my sons will choose and that we would regret it."

I nodded like crazy, comforted Lisa, and told her that the AEA teacher did not know Deaf culture. Deaf kids with Deaf parents have mutual ties to Deaf culture because they share the same language. Lisa nodded silently.

Suddenly, an idea popped in my head, "Why don't you file due process against that AEA teacher?"

Monday, May 23

It was the last few days before the end of the school year. The students were helping the adults take down posters and art from the walls.

When the students went out for their lunch break, I found the opportunity to ask Mrs. Jones about my future employment with Knight School.

"So far, we think the school will cut two and a half hours from your work," she said.

Her reply did not surprise me. There had already been rumors circulating about my hours. I was not sure who decided to cut my hours, the principal or Mrs. Jones. I emailed Mrs. Jones and the principal about the matter, expecting a similar generic response. Instead, they pointed their fingers at each other.

During recess, I walked into Mrs. Feldman's classroom and talked to her about the issues with my reduced hours. I wanted to know if she would have a problem with the new hours. She said that she was fine with it.

Mrs. Feldman has an inability to deal with difficult students. I curiously mused to myself how she would handle Emma in the fall.

After the discussion with Mrs. Feldman and Mrs. Jones, I took Emma and Toby to the gym for their lessons. The gym teacher had the students play on the basketball court. The gym teacher and Kallie gathered at the corner of the gym and started talking. I focused my attention on Emma.

Out of the corner of my eye, I saw Kallie's extreme hand movements. Eavesdropping into her gesticulated conversation, I could not believe what I was seeing. She was discussing a bikini contest from the night before! The fifth-grade hearing teacher was the judge of this particular contest, and Kallie had been helping her friend to win.

I eavesdropped some more to make sure I was seeing what I was seeing, but Kallie gestured for me to join the conversation.

"I helped my best friend win the contest. I stood behind her and helped her untie the lace. Once she ripped off the bikini top, I grabbed her boobs and juggled them in front of the guys and Mr. Bryant!"

An overwhelming sinking sensation hit my stomach.

Kallie was talking into the microphones around the gym teacher's neck! The deaf students could be hearing everything she said.

Pointing at the microphones, I hastily told her to stop the conversation.

Kallie looked at the gym teacher as he picked up the microphones.

In unison they said, "Oops!"

Kallie quickly justified her poor choice of topics:

"They don't know what I'm talking about. You know, deaf kids. Know nothing," she said, using her hand to make an 'O' shape slamming it to her forehead.

She ended our conversation with a smug grin. It made me sick knowing she was working with deaf children.

Friday, May 27

The Knight teachers had been planning a retirement party for the principal for several days. I didn't know much about it because I had been busy with Emma and had not had time to engage in such plans. The interpreters are not required to give me details about anything, so I did not expect them to divulge the retirement party plans to me.

Some of the teachers and all of the interpreters decorated the principal's five-wheeled swivel chair with the theme of a fast hot rod car. They covered it with posters, stickers, glitters and streamers. A couple of weeks before, the principal had broken his ankle, and he had been using the chair to scoot across the floor.

Several of the staff was in the hallway with a camcorder when the principal scooted down the hall toward Mrs. Jones' room at super speed. The people in the hallway cheered and took pictures of him with streamers flying around his thighs.

He stormed into Mrs. Jones' room and demanded to know where Emma was. I pointed at the floor where she lay fast asleep. The principal seemed baffled.

"She's napping?!"

"Yes, she's been napping for a while," I said. Puzzled, I asked him why.

He asked me whether Emma got into a fight. I replied that she hadn't.

Everyone gathered around the door to get the principal's confused and panicked attention. As he turned to look at the cheering crowd in the doorway, they all said, "Gotcha! Happy retirement!"

Immediately Emma's body jerked and she woke up.

Several of the people pointed their cameras and camcorders at the principal.

Later that day, one of the interpreters told me that the principal had been tricked into helping her restrain Emma so that they could surprise him. I found the idea of using a special needs child to trick someone to be demeaning and beneath my standards.

For quite some time I had felt that the school was using Emma for inappropriate reasons, on a much larger scale than tricking someone to come to a party.

Emma should have been in a much more appropriate educational environment from the beginning. She has problems of such magnitude that they are way out of the AEA's scope. Her disability is more profound than just her deafness. But why would they keep her in the deaf classroom rather than move her to someplace more appropriate for students with a wider range of disorders?

Then it occurred to me, the school district receives a certain amount of money, per student, when they assign a student with disability to a school in their district. I'm just sayin'…

"The definition of insanity is repeating the same mistakes over and over again and expecting different results."

Albert Einstein

FIFTH SEASON

Fall 2005, pre-planning week

At the last outdoor event hosted by the Deaf Club, I learned that Ritch's mother Brenda and her Deaf partner, along with Chad and Lisa, had sent their children to the Deaf school. It was a good thing that they had never considered sending their kids to Knight school.

I was pleased to learn that Allen, the boy who was featured in the news for his CI, continued to do well at his home school. He was the only deaf child there. The only interpreter service he had was an AEA itinerant. A teacher for the deaf, a speech therapist, trainers (the devices, not people) and microphones for his listening assistance were Allen's only support. I wondered if he had any friends.

When I arrived home, I found two letters from Knight school in my mailbox. One of them was an employment letter. I tore it open and read it. I was to give up two and a half hours per day, dropping from six and a half hours to four hours. The second letter said that there would be an open house and that all the teachers wanted me there. Attending this event was purely voluntary, but I thought it would be good to go and find out what new changes had been decided for the school during the summer break.

At the open house, I went to Mrs. Feldman's classroom. The new principal introduced himself and continued on his way, greeting the deaf students.

"He has no idea what it is like here?" I quietly thought to myself.

I moved on to look at the names of the students on the desks. My eyes nearly popped out when I saw Dalton's name on one of the desks. I asked Kallie, Cassie and Lauren if Dalton was back, and they said that he was.

They also told me that Carmen the interpreter had transferred to the D/HH program at a local High School that also provided D/HH inclusive program for deaf students attending there.

All fourth graders had been assigned to their regular homeroom teachers. Emma, Joey and Toby had been assigned to Mrs. Diaz's room, and Alyssa, Brendan and Dalton had been moved to Mrs. Taylor's room. This seemed to be a good idea. Joey and Dalton had a history of conflict, whereas Dalton and Toby used to always team up and leave Joey isolated in the hearing classes.

Because of all the time I had spent upstairs, I didn't know any of the other new deaf students, just Kayla and Rhett. I reconciled myself to the notion that it would be a nice change of scenery to be working in Mrs. Feldman's classroom with shortened hours.

Mrs. Feldman had all of us sit down. She explained that she would be the Interpreter for the fifth-grade class. She said that Kallie would be with me in Mrs. Diaz's class and that Cassie would be in Mrs. Taylor's room.

"Libby, I want you to stay here until one o'clock to get Emma acquainted. You'll supervise her during her lunch."

I had asked Mrs. Feldman specifically to put me and Cassie together because of her top-notch sign language skills. I did not want to work with Kallie because of her shameful work ethics and her inferior sign language skills.

"Ask Joey, he'll tell you he wants Cassie," I implored. She wouldn't change it.

Upset with the assignments, I asked Mrs. Feldman if I could leave before the rest of the parents and students showed up. She handed me a list of the names and grades of the students and I left.

One new family I noticed on my way out included a red-haired girl wearing two BTEs and a pair of prescription eyeglasses. The child clung to her mother's waist as I passed. I did not think anything about it. As far as I was concerned, the open house was over.

Tuesday, August 23

It was the first day of school. Two of the interpreters and I escorted three deaf students to their new hearing classroom. Emma, Joey, Toby and I together entered the classroom. The teacher introduced herself as Mrs. Diaz, a 4th grade teacher.

Mrs. Diaz had all of the students sit in a circle on a large area rug near her desk. Mrs. Diaz explained her expectations, classroom rules, and lesson plans.

There were four islands of six desks that faced each other. There was a seventh desk that faced the two rows of six desks. The island nearest the door had Emma's desk. In the event that Emma acted inappropriately, I could easily get her out of the classroom with the least amount of disruption.

Joey and Toby sat with five of their hearing classmates in the large circle.

On the area rug, Mrs. Diaz instructed all of the students to introduce themselves, their names, hobbies, what they did over the summer and what they hoped to learn during the year. Joey and Toby slithered further back from the circle.

Mrs. Diaz held up a microphone and explained to the class that Emma, Joey and Toby were hearing impaired and that the microphone was one of the tools that helped them to hear. She told them to speak directly into the microphone. Joey and Toby squirmed uncomfortably. They were extremely embarrassed. They looked around to see if anyone was staring at them.

A boy went first and spoke awkwardly into the microphone and it caused squelching feedback. The class broke out in hysterical giggles. The deaf boys looked at each other constantly, probably trying to subconsciously reassure each other. Mrs. Diaz quickly fixed the feedback and told the students to hold the microphone slightly away from their mouths. After the first boy finished his introduction, the mic was passed along to the right.

This took quite a while because there were 28 students in the class all-in-all. The closer the mic got to Emma, the more nervous she became.

"What I talk about?" She asked me.

I helped her recall what she had done over the summer and her nervousness turned into excitement when it was almost her turn. The student on Emma's left finished introducing herself and reached around skipping Emma to give the mic to the student on Emma's right. Mrs. Diaz did not notice that the girl had skipped Emma.

At the end of the introductions, Mrs. Diaz looked at Emma and yelled, making a scene:

"Oh my gosh! I forgot you!"

She quickly trotted over to Emma and handed her the microphone. As I should have expected, Emma licked the microphone and shoved the peanut sized device in her mouth. The students next to her scooted away so that their knees were no longer touching. After Emma introduced herself, she tried to hand the wet mic to the girl on her right, who was gagging.

I quickly told Emma that the girl had already introduced herself. I took the microphone out of her hand and returned it to Mrs. Diaz.

As the class started their next activity, the students were to write in their journals. After 10 minutes of writing, each student was to read to the other students in the same island to encourage a community effort of sharing and listening.

It had been a few days of school, and I had noticed that everyone wrote in their journals except Toby. I watched Toby's island and saw several students read their journals. When it was Toby's turn to speak, he spoke, but I could not read his lips. However, I knew that he was not even looking at his journal, because it was closed and tucked away in his hands.

A hearing girl next to him said something that made him shake his head negatively. Then, she grabbed Toby's journal from his hands. The girl spoke to him again. Still struggling, he clutched onto his journal, wringing it, so that it would not expose his chicken scratches in the place of penmanship.

The girl talked over Toby, constantly interrupting him. He started to get visibly upset. Several of the classmates on his island started to giggle. Toby kept tugging on his journal while it was in the girl's grips.

There was Kallie chatting with Mrs. Diaz at her desk, so I became concerned and started to go to them.

Suddenly, Toby elbowed the girl, and she immediately freed his journal.

"You're stupid and I hate you!" She said rubbing her arm.

This was the third year that Toby was put on the spot. There were similar incidents each of the two years prior. The previous year, the same girl read Toby's journal during circle time and said that she could not understand it. The girl had pointed to the illegible scribble in his journal.

Toby had learned to rescue himself by distracting his listeners with exaggerated tales of fascinating adventures in order to spare himself humiliation. He was quite a great storyteller. I knew he was going to get away with a lot.

Me, on the other hand, I was going to have a lot more trouble before it was over.

Monday, August 29

This was my third year working at Knight Elementary School as a one-on-one communicative assistant for the deaf and developmentally challenged girl, Emma. She had pinched me, pulled my hair, spit on me, bitten me, tripped me, stapled my finger and clothes, and stabbed me, other students and teachers with scissors, sharpened pencils and thumbtacks.

Emma had ripped the name plaques from doors, deliberately coughed and spat in people's food, and called them inappropriate names. She had threatened to bring her BB gun to school and shoot me with it. She was often let go with a warning or at most, time out from recess.

As a fourth grader, she was now with a different D/HH teacher, Mrs. Feldman. This year, Emma was almost as tall as I was. She had become difficult for me to handle physically. Mrs. Feldman overheard her telling me that she would bring her BB gun to school and shoot me with it. She sent Emma to the principal's office, but the principal, however, was new.

To my horror, the new principal sent Emma back to the classroom with only a warning. When I asked Mrs. Feldman and the principal why discipline was not being implemented, they said that she is a special needs child. We have to go through the IEP protocol, because the IEP does not allow us to use the standard disciplinary techniques that are used on the hearing students.

Emma knew exactly what she was doing! She was only behaving inappropriately because the educational placement still did not meet her needs.

Shortly after Emma returned from the principal's office, she whacked my head with a four inch thick dictionary. I bypassed the D/HH teacher and took her directly to the principal's office myself.

The principal called Emma's mother so that she could handle her. Emma's mother agreed to take away her Gameboy, TV, computer and BB gun privileges. Through the speaker phone, where everyone in the principal's office could hear it, she told her daughter that the items would be on *top* of the refrigerator. Smart move Mom...

Friday, September 2

I asked Emma if she had played with the restricted items. She said yeah. I asked her a tricky question:

"Were they still on top of the refrigerator?"

"No, I still had them," she said enthusiastically.

The kid still had full access to the restricted items! Really?!

First thing in the morning, Mrs. Diaz lectured about new writing assignments for the journals. She said that she would pick assorted topics from the raffle basket, and the students were to write at least two paragraphs or a page of creative writing. During the whole time Mrs. Diaz was talking, Kallie translated, but Joey was not paying attention.

As soon as Mrs. Diaz had finished talking, she picked a topic from the basket and read off the paper strip in her hand:

"If you saw your friend stealing things from the school, what would you do and why?"

163

All the students started writing in their journals while Joey stared ahead. Toby fiddled with objects on his desk, knowing that he could not read or write. Emma panicked and started bawling. My job was to rescue her, then reassure her and bring her focus back to the topic. I ended up dictating her writing to her — as I had done since I began working with her. In 25 minutes, she managed one sentence, "Stealing is wrong."

Kallie walked over to Joey and reminded him to take the journal from his desk, open it, get a pencil and start writing.

"I don't know what to write," Joey said.

"I told you three times," Kallie replied. "About stealing, what would you do? Now, that's the fourth time I've told you."

Kallie slammed her fingers down on Joey's desk and yelled, "Now write!" With tight lips, she stood and stared at Joey.

It was quite intimidating. There was an uncomfortable period of silence.

"Where's your daughter? I don't see her around here anymore?" I asked her.

Kallie inched closer to me and explained, "Mrs. Weaver refuses to take my kid into her class because of me. What's more, the principal refuses to let my kid into Mr. Paynes' class too," she said.

"Why?" I inquired.

"Because if one of the interpreters is absent, and I am the only one available to interpret for Timmy... If my kid stayed in Mr. Paynes' class where Timmy is now, that would create a conflict. So, that is why I sent my kid back to her home school district where I live."

Just as the adults took the students to the cafeteria for their lunch, the new principal decided that there would be changes made around the cafeteria. He ordered all the students to line up, take their tray of food, and to sit in one row, single file, rather than pick whichever seat they wanted.

Once a bench was filled, they had to sit at the next available table. All the students faced the west side of the cafeteria, one row per table; the opposite rows in front of them on the same table were to remain unoccupied.

That created a problem for the deaf students. If they did not stand together in line, then they would be inadvertently seated separately. Hearing students had their friends on their sides, while the deaf students sat between the hearing students. The hearing students had someone to talk to; the deaf students had no one.

A hearing boy asked Dalton something. Dalton smiled, played with his food, and made a face. The boy asked him something again, Dalton replied in shrugs. The hearing boy gave up and talked to the hearing boy next to him.

Joey looked around apprehensively and fiddled with his utensils. The hearing students on his sides were talking to each other across Joey's food tray. When one of the hearing students said something to Joey, he stared straight ahead pretending to not see the kid talking.

The cafeteria was loud and the adults on duty wore the microphones – and they were reserved strictly for the adults. If the deaf students had them, then the lunch experience probably would have been better. Or if they had the deaf students sit together, in the Deaf row, as Joey would have liked.

The lunch seating arrangement was inappropriate to the maximum extent of the LRE mandate; and, in fact, it created the *most restrictive* environment. Everything that was set up for Joey actually worked against Joey, as it did for most of the deaf students here. He didn't have the maximum access to *information*. The deaf students and Joey stared at their peers' backsides as they ate. The adults on duty were indiscriminately talking into the AEA microphones. The cafeteria walls were absent of posters and banners. In addition, there was a lack of eye contact with anyone in the cafeteria room. Zero input and zero output.

The disciplinary methods applied at the Deaf schools in the 80's were somewhat similar to the cafeteria seating arrangement at Knight, the single row table. One of the disciplinary measures at the Deaf schools was that the Deaf students would be placed in an isolating environment such as a dimmed corner, facing against the wall. That's the basic idea of 'zero input/output'.

The Knight principal inadvertently punished the innocent deaf students, by depriving them of input, socially and linguistically.

I confronted the principal about this arrangement and I reminded him that this single row approach worked well for those who shared one common language. He replied that this was a way to break up cliques and to force others to learn to respect whoever sat with them.

It was pointless to continue.

Monday, September 5

The previous Friday, Kallie, Cassie and Lauren had checked all the trainers, microphones and tele-loop devices to ensure that all the expensive equipment was working properly. All of the equipment had been accounted for. One of the pieces from Toby's tele-loop device was missing on Monday. Toby was notoriously careless with his tele-loop device. He intentionally lost or broke the pieces of the device so that he could get out of having to wear the embarrassing object around his neck.

I had warned both Mrs. Feldman and the audiologist about this early on. The devices created an obstacle to Toby's mobility. During recess or gym class, the tele-loop device would fall from his shirt pocket or from around his neck and break into pieces. The cord was not long enough for him to tuck the processor into his pants pocket, so it hung heavily on his shirt. I could see why he thought this was a useless piece of junk — and he had already had to use it for three years.

Tuesday, September 6

Mrs. Diaz found the missing piece of tele-loop in the back corner of the bathroom. Toby probably knew about the missing piece and had gone without a listening device for the whole day on purpose, because he had gone into the bathroom before Mrs. Diaz found the piece.

With that in mind, it would have been easy enough to pin the blame on Toby. However, this issue had been repeatedly reported to the therapists with nothing done about it. His behavior was a sign that he did not like it. If it were up to me, I would have gotten him new hearing aids more compatible with the trainers or something with better access.

Emma behaved inappropriately in Mrs. Diaz's classroom, so I took her back to Mrs. Feldman's room. Mrs. Feldman was in the room alone. Handling Emma would be completely up to me because Mrs. Feldman seemed to be busy. I went over to the board games and chose a jigsaw puzzle that Emma liked. As I pulled out a jigsaw puzzle box, memories of Emma and the board games flashed in my mind.

During my first year with Emma, Mrs. Jones had warned me to not let her put away the board games. I ignored Mrs. Jones' warning and let Emma do this particular chore herself, presuming she was a big girl now.

Just as Emma had packed away the game, she rapidly ripped the cardboard box into pieces.

I should have listened.

In my second year with Emma, I watched her more closely as she collected the games into the cardboard boxes. She got up from the floor with the box in her hands.

"Wow! What an improvement!" I thought.

Boy, was I wrong! Half way across the room, she bit into the jigsaw puzzle box, ripped it all up and threw the torn pieces into the air. The pieces of torn box and puzzles fell all over the place like confetti at a New Year party.

As usual, Mrs. Jones did not do anything. She simply told Emma to clean up the mess and put the game on the table. That was it. No disciplinary action was taken.

I stopped reminiscing, looked at the jigsaw puzzle box and wondered if she would do the same thing this year. She definitely could not be trusted.

As she connected the pieces of puzzle, I noticed that her fine motor skills and speed had improved tremendously.

Mrs. Feldman interrupted her and said, "Oh good! You've done very well! It's time to clean up and put the games back on the shelf."

I immediately started cleaning up after Emma. Mrs. Feldman stopped me. She wanted Emma to clean them up herself.

Behind Emma's back I protested, "She will destroy the box."

167

Mrs. Feldman shook her head and said, "It's fine. She won't do that because we are watching her."

Emma got up from her seat and grabbed the cheaply made cardboard box, gripping it tighter and tighter. The box began to cave. Her knuckles were turning white. Preparing for her unwanted behavior, I inched closer and placed my hand on Emma's shoulder. Mrs. Feldman saw this and told me to back off.

I did what I was told, and instantly, all of the jigsaw pieces flew into the air, landing in all directions.

Her speed, precision, and coordinated abilities had improved indeed!

Maybe the next time, Mrs. Feldman would listen to me.

Friday, September 9

I walked into Mrs. Feldman's room and spotted one of the deaf students' worksheets. They chose the assignments that they disliked the least. For one of the worksheets, the deaf students were to choose the best sounds from a box, and match them up to the picture that most closely represented that sound.

There were pictures of six bears making different noises:

"Ding – Dong"

"Vroom"

"ZZZZ"

"Rat-tat-tat"

"Splash"

"Snap"

These were books from a popular phonics website. The book was at level G, for students 6 to 7 years old. Phonics has done wonders for unskilled readers, but it was a whole different story for deaf students.

In disbelief, I stared at the worksheet. This kind of work made no sense — these students are *deaf*! The "ZZZZ" sound is impossible to hear. The children were pleasing the teacher instead of learning. None of the students knew what "Splash" sounded like. The deaf children have to take off their hearing aids when they are exposed to any activity having to do with water, thus, disabling their hearing.

After being asked what "Splash" meant, I explained that it meant something falling into water, making that sound. They looked at me and asked for more information, so I led them to the public sink and showed them what "Splash" sounded like.

"Oh, that's splash!" One of the deaf students exclaimed.

They thought the word "Splash" had a definition and did not realize that it meant a certain sound was created.

I asked Mrs. Feldman how this book got into the school program. Mrs. Feldman explained that her best friend, a resource room teacher, had discovered the phonics program online and recommended it to the school district; the school district had immediately implemented the program district-wide. "Best friend" were the key words right there.

Tuesday, September 13

Toby pretended to forget his journals (notebooks with blank, lined pages) at home, but he actually left them in Mrs. Feldman's classroom. It was an evasive tactic he used so that he could get out of doing his writing assignments. He had a spare journal in Mrs. Diaz's room, discreetly tucked away.

Kallie and Mrs. Diaz quizzed him about the responsibility of bringing his journal to class.

"I left it at home," He said.

"No, he has the original journal in his backpack in Mrs. Feldman's classroom, and he has a spare one tucked away in his desk," I interrupted.

The women immediately bent down and searched through the accumulated filth and junk in Toby's desk to find the hidden journal.

While the students were doing their assigned writing, I read Mrs. Diaz's lips as she complained to Kallie about Joey's overbearing parents.

Apparently, Joey's parents had come into her classroom twice that month with a sound technician to evaluate the noise disturbance. The parents wanted to lower the ceiling in the bathroom and the coat room area because the noise echoed.

Deaf students are easily distracted by noises (common sounds to hearing people are strange to deaf people). Sounds that hearing students can easily block out are intriguing to deaf students. It would be the equivalent of a hearing student's response to an extremely bright light, a suddenly cold draft or the sudden smell of smoke — the hearing child would naturally want to know the source of the light, the cold or the smoke.

Stimulus that is constantly there is easy to ignore, while the same stimulus experienced intermittently becomes a curiosity. Deaf kids with some degree of hearing ability are easily distracted by those noises which they can still actually hear. Background clamors can cause other sounds to become garbled. Sounds which may be distinctive in a quiet room can become a collage of indeterminable noises when jumbled in together with the reverberations of background commotion.

Joey's parents wanted the ceiling lowered in the bathroom and the coatroom area because sounds echoed.

Naturally, Mrs. Diaz disagreed, "I don't teach in that bathroom or coatroom!" She said pointing to the back of the room.

Mrs. Diaz complained that Joey's parents emailed her frequently during the day, taking her attention away from her lesson preparation time. She also rejected the parents' request to put tennis balls on the tips of the chair legs to reduce the scuffing noises.

"No way! This is my class and I don't want to see 120 bright yellow tennis balls on the floor. I will get felt caps instead." Mrs. Diaz exclaimed.

I thought the tennis balls were a great idea, since they would last longer than felt caps.

Friday, September 16

Just as Emma and I walked into Mrs. Diaz's room, I noticed two construction workers taking away ladders, tools, and material from the bathroom and coat room in the back of her classroom.

While staring at the workers, I felt someone tapping on my shoulder. I turned around to see Mrs. Diaz and Kallie. Mrs. Diaz spoke to Kallie, who relayed Mrs. Diaz's message.

"The men are almost finished with adding the soundproof tiles in the back room. Don't let Emma in there until all of the materials are gone," Mrs. Diaz reminded me.

Kallie and I crept inside the coatroom to peek at the new ceiling and soundproof walls. The new ceiling felt unnaturally close to my head.

"It feels like it'll fall down on my head, and the walls don't look durable. It looks punchable." I said.

Kallie chuckled, "By the way, the ceiling was moved down some feet lower, and Mrs. Diaz said that it cost the school over $4,000!"

"Just to lower the ceiling and soundproof the walls because of echo noise?" I asked.

Kallie nodded, signing, "Yeah, that's awful. Joey's parents even hired a lawyer, so the school administrators caved. They don't understand that Joey is only in here to go to the bathroom or to hang up his coat and backpack."

The school funds would have been better spent to buy extra trainers, CI loaners, provide backup interpreters, closed caption devices, and so many promised services that it lacked.

* * *

After two tough weeks of working with Emma in the afternoons, Mrs. Feldman spoke to the principal about giving me more hours to work with her. My main duties were to prevent inappropriate behavior, dictate Emma's assignments, to assist communication between Emma and the staff, reducing or removing stressors, and comforting Emma. This is a shadowing, role-modeling job.

Emma had been acting inappropriately by eating crayons and throwing things across the room, because the stressors were getting too much for her. Mrs. Feldman came to Mrs. Diaz's room to observe her. After a few minutes, Mrs. Feldman left.

I complained to Kallie about my duties and the length of Mrs. Feldman's observation.

Kallie replied, "Mrs. Feldman feels out of place in this classroom. She prefers to be in her own classroom because she knows the concept of mainstreaming deaf kids is messed up. What's more, Toby cannot read or write. Did you see Mrs. Feldman's facial expression when she read Toby's journal? It read, 'dab cau wht mga cpr har'. The letters weren't even on the lines!" She stuck her tongue out, crossed her eyes and mimed the writing all over the page.

It dawned on me that she was right. Mrs. Feldman rarely showed interest and was not actively involved with difficult deaf students. She dumped them off on the interpreters who were unprepared to educate the deaf students themselves. She was delinquent and avoided responsibility.

Kallie informed me that Emma cried during the social studies class the previous afternoon. The whole time Kallie was talking to me, she did not interpret for the deaf students.

"I comforted her and explained to the classmates that Emma is different. The classmates murmured, 'Yeah, we know'."

Kallie did not realize that they had known Emma since the second grade. I looked at Emma and asked her why she cried.

Kallie grabbed my attention and said, "She cried *real* loud."

Emma hit my arm to get my attention, so I looked at her again. "I want in Mrs. Feldman room all day. Don't like here!"

Kallie and I looked at each other. She wanted to be in "deaf self-contained classroom" *all-day*. However, the LRE mandate went against Emma's wishes.

Emma was forced against her will to interact with peers who spoke and moved too quickly for her to stay caught up. This was the frustrating aspect for her. She often behaved at her best when she was in the Deaf classroom, but the LRE mandate didn't allow her to have this choice. Had her home school district hired a one-on-one assistant and allowed her to have daily naps, then it would have been doable. She even wouldn't have had to be stuck in AEA van for an hour without any peer interaction. She could have spent more time with her brothers, as she would have liked.

Later that night, I stopped by a local gym to work out. While I was there, a young deaf friend of mine came by. She told me about a new interpreter at her high school. I asked her what the interpreter's name was.

"Carmen," she signed.

Kallie had wanted that job, but Carmen got the dibs on it, because she had been teaching sign language to the top dogs at the school board.

Monday, September 19

Mrs. Feldman was giving an explanation on how to do an assignment. She signed the word 'light' (as in light bulb) for a coloring task, "Color them in 'light' (light bulb) blue."

She signed differently than Mrs. Jones. Mrs. Jones would sign the word 'light' (as in lightweight) for ceiling light. "Please turn on the 'lights' (lightweight)." Semantically, it did not make any sense.

My thoughts went back to the students' assignments. I spotted a sound-test chart (phonics) on the table. I wondered what they were really for, since I had only seen Mrs. Feldman use them two years before for her Mastery of Phonics certification.

Mrs. Feldman picked up a phonics chart and showed the deaf students how to read the lettered symbols and pronounce them correctly. They were to echo during and after Mrs. Feldman's phonetic prompt. Alyssa was to go first. Mrs. Feldman pointed to the symbol and Alyssa pronounced it aloud. When Alyssa mispronounced the sound, Mrs. Feldman repeated it. Alyssa mimicked the sound, watching the disappointed expression on Mrs. Feldman's face. Alyssa broke down crying.

The deaf students became really stressed. Some of them quickly glanced around the room, others thumped their pencils on the table, and the rest laid their heads down in frustration. There was no way to escape the sound-test chart.

After brief rounds of phonetic prompts, Mrs. Feldman started the new spelling words for the week. She turned on the overhead projector and wrote one word at a time. She gave the definitions and instructed the students to make up a sentence using the new word.

A few words into the list, Mrs. Feldman wrote the word 'neuer.' I knew that she meant 'never' but her 'v' did not have a prominent point. Mrs. Feldman spoke the word 'never' aloud and emphasized the 'v' sound. Within my peripheral vision, I saw the students' pencils moving, so I looked more closely at a couple of their papers. The students copied the word as it was from the projector — 'neuer'.

Phonics had been so overemphasized in the classroom that the students copied Mrs. Feldman's poor penmanship, thinking that this was how the word should be spelled, rather than using their deaf ears to discern the phonetic sounds.

Mrs. Feldman saw that the children had written 'neuer' on their papers and tried to correct them. But the deaf students had a good comeback. A few of them yelled simultaneously.

In ASL grammar/mode, "Why me too? You have *[written a]* 'u'," Alyssa pointed to the obvious proof of her assertions still in evidence on the screen on the wall, and basked in the signed sentiments of approval and agreement from the other students.

Phonics was failing the deaf students because it confused them about how to spell words correctly. With the lack of communication at home, hours of speech therapy and unskilled signers (teachers, interpreters, and speech therapists), phonics was just another way of beating around the bush for these students, creating many useless and frustrating "make-work" projects to waste time and run down the clock.

Wednesday, September 21

The gym teacher had taken Mrs. Diaz's class out to the soccer field. While he explained the rules of the game to the students, the adults stood at the sideline of the field. Somehow, I got stuck holding jackets, books and other items that weighted me down. Emma had been behaving herself, but I was still watching her closely.

I felt a tap on my shoulder. It was the gym teacher, asking me if I was going to run with Emma around the field.

174

"No, she's not hurting anyone right now," I replied.

Kallie asked me why not. I quickly looked at the gym teacher to see if he had asked me that question — he had not.

With my arms full of items, signing would have been ineffectual.

I fingerspelled T-I-R-E-D because I was tired of still holding onto all of those items and couldn't drop them just to chase Emma. Kallie did not quite catch my spelling, so I repeated it slower.

Kallie had an 'aha' moment and mouthed the words, "Got it." She then went and told the gym teacher, "She said she is 'top heavy'," grabbing her own chest.

"Ugh," I cringed. "That conversation was between you and me. He did not ask you that question, and you should not have gotten him involved!"

"Well, the teachers around here do not like it if the signers sign in front of them without explaining. It makes them feel like they are being talked about," she replied.

I rolled my eyes at the hypocrisy of her statement, because the hearing people around here talk in front of the deaf people all the time, without an explanation too.

Aside from this, Kallie had violated interpreting ethics. If I had wanted the gym teacher to know what I was saying, I would have told him myself or allowed the gym teacher to initiate the conversation with me first. In spite of receiving her community college sign language interpreter training, as a hearing person, Kallie was still unacquainted with many if not most "Deaf culture" social etiquettes.

* * *

"None so deaf as those that will not hear."

Matthew Henry, paraphrasing Jeremiah 5:21,
Ezekiel 12:2 & Matthew 13:12

The speech therapist came in every Wednesday at about noon. Lauren and I chatted as Mrs. Feldman had the deaf students arrange the seating in a circular view so that they could see each other.

Lauren complained about the speech therapist's anti-sign language attitude. Recently, the speech therapist opposed Lauren and the deaf students' use of iconic sign to replace written words in a book.

The speech therapist had casually observed Lauren reading a book with Zeke, when Zeke had come across a problem understanding one of the words. The interpreter signed the word 'tree' to give Zeke a nudge forward.

After Zeke threw out a few random words, she had patiently said, "Look at the signed word and tell me what it resembles. Try to visualize what I am showing you."

Then she had emphasized the iconic sign of a tree.

"Tree!" Zeke excitedly yelled out and continued reading the book.

At the end of the reading assignment, the speech therapist had walked up to Lauren and had scolded her for using iconic signs:

"American Sign Language is not a visual language," the therapist had said.

"Ouch!" I thought. That stung. That amount of knee-jerk, pompous, ignorant hubris and blatantly oblivious disregard for the obvious truth actually hurt my brain!

Lauren had tried using SEE 2, and it had failed to help Zeke understand the simple word "Tree." ASL had. At least Lauren was getting it, even if the therapist wasn't.

Back in the classroom, I felt a tap on my shoulder.

"Emma needs you to shadow her," Mrs. Feldman gently reminded me.

I quickly went over to Emma to monitor the stressors surrounding her.

The speech therapist was moderating a dialogue game. She asked each student one question, and the student had to answer the question correctly using his or her best spoken English grammar while signing the word in SEE simultaneously, i.e. SimCom (simultaneous communication).

176

It was Alyssa's turn to answer. She signed the word 'hurt' in perfect ASL. The speech therapist did not understand her, so she asked her to repeat. Alyssa raised her foot and rested it on the chair. This time, she voiced and repeated the word in perfect ASL on her raised knee, a localized sign.

The speech therapist asked me what Alyssa had signed.

"She signed 'hurt'," I voiced to the therapist.

"I've never seen that sign before," she said, "Is that correct SEE 2?"

I knew that she knew the sign was not one of the SEE approved signs.

"She signed that in ASL. I understood her," I replied.

The speech therapist immediately consulted the infamous yellow SEE book and found the SEE approved sign for 'hurt.' She immediately criticized Alyssa's choice of the signed word. I instantly cringed — ASL was Alyssa's native language and the sign that she had used was in fact an ASL approved sign.

SEE 2 was designed for *hearing people's benefit* and is not used in the Deaf community as a main means of communication. Hearing people, educators particularly, simply didn't want to learn a new language, ASL. Correcting a deaf student on the correct use of signed words (especially when the student uses the correct sign in her native language of ASL) is worse than an English speaker correcting the native speaker of Swahili (who in fact used the correct word in her native language of Swahili), insisting that the English word is correct and the Swahili word is wrong — while they are both in Africa!

Helping deaf children to engage in meaningful communication is far more important than rigidly following school policy and the hearing teachers' preferred method of sign — SEE 2. Avenues must be explored to find the communication that makes the most sense to the deaf individual and the Deaf community.

Friday, September 23

The PTA helped to organize a Jump-A-Thon to raise money for the school. Everyone was excited about the event. The deaf students helped put up posters and flyers and wore Jump-A-Thon tee shirts.

The event was held on the soccer field across the street from the school. Upon the students' arrival, the leader of the event talked about safety and performed warm-up exercises. The leader sent the fourth graders to the designated snack area. The D/HH teachers led the deaf students to the blacktop to look for their stands (tables) for meet-up. The snack tables were separated by classes and marked with the teachers' names.

The interpreters inquired about Mrs. Feldman's table. One of the PTA moms gasped and covered her mouth. She quickly looked at one of the PTA moms nearby.

"We forgot about them!" She shrieked.

"Are there enough bottles and snacks from the other tables that they could share with us?" One of the interpreters asked.

"Nope… Each kid third grade and up only gets one bottle and one snack. Sorry." One of the PTA moms callously answered.

We were mortified. Brendan, one of the deaf students in the fourth grade, had numerous health problems. Without plenty of fluids, he would have to sit this one out. The hurtful and confusing part was that most of the hearing students had deaf classmates in their hearing classes, on their roster.

As bad as it was, the deaf students had a great attitude and went ahead with the Jump-A-Thon.

One of the PTA leaders promised to provide goodies on Monday to make up for the mistake.

Emma did not fare so well at the event. She tossed her microphone up in the air and caught it. Mrs. Feldman warned her to quit doing that and tried to retrieve the device from her. Emma apologized and promised not to do it again.

Emma had been asking me if her parents were going to show up. I had no clue, but remembered the last Jump-A-Thon, when her grandparents showed up; appearing embarrassed to be seen with Emma. I offered to be Emma's partner again, but she shoved me away from her. I stood about six feet behind her this time.

As soon as Mrs. Feldman walked away, Emma threw her microphone up into the air again. I tried to reach her in time, but I was not quite fast enough. Emma caught the microphone and smashed it to pieces on the sidewalk.

I wanted so badly to tell Mrs. Feldman, "I told you so."

When Emma realized what she had done, she apologized profusely to me.

"I'm the wrong person to apologize to," I told her. "You need to apologize to Mrs. Feldman."

I turned to look for Mrs. Feldman, but she had already moved far ahead. At the top of my lungs, I screamed out her name. Mrs. Feldman turned around and looked at us. Emma signed repeatedly, "Sorry."

Mrs. Feldman jogged toward us and saw the broken pieces of microphone in Emma's hands and on the sidewalk. She asked Emma why she did that.

"Don't like jump," Emma nervously replied.

That part was true, but I knew that there was more to it than that. "What else?" I asked.

"Mom and Dad not here! I mad." Tears flowed down her cheeks as she sobbed. Then she collapsed on the ground and started pulling out chunks of grass.

Monday, September 26

I arrived at school and checked the teachers' lounge to see if the PTA had lived up to its promise. There were goodies and water bottles on one of the circular tables. The snacks were nicer than the snacks that had been offered on Friday.

I grabbed some of the goodies and water bottles on my way out and went next door to Mrs. Feldman's room.

"Hey! Did you see what the PTA brought for all of us?" I asked.

179

Mrs. Feldman and the interpreters smiled.

I got a nagging feeling in the pit of my stomach. Something was wrong. I scanned the classroom for goodies and water bottles for the students. There were none in sight.

"Where are the goodies for the students?" I asked one of the staff.

"They didn't provide any for the students, just for the adults," Mrs. Feldman shook her head.

The deaf students would never have the chance to enjoy the same benefits as their hearing classmates! I went back into the teachers' lounge and stole enough snacks and water bottles to sneak into the students' backpacks.

Later that morning, while Emma was taking her nap, I asked Mrs. Feldman about the future of Emma's education.

"Will Emma be here next year for the fifth grade?" I asked.

"Her parents want her back in their home district next fall," Mrs. Feldman said, looking up from what she was doing. "They are hoping that we can rehabilitate her in time for her to be independent."

Taken aback by her response, I swallowed the wrong way. It hurt my throat and caused me to cough.

"What do you think? Will she be able to show that she is capable of being self-sufficient in school?" someone asked.

"If they do take her out, it won't surprise me if they bring her back," Mrs. Feldman shrugged.

That was definitely not the answer I was expecting.

Tuesday, September 27

First thing in the morning, Mrs. Feldman had a conference with all of the room interpreters and me. She informed us that a new student, Nathalie, would be joining us.

"Is that the same girl that came with her mother to the open house; the one with dark red-hair, freckles and glasses?" One of the interpreters asked.

Mrs. Feldman affirmed, but she cautioned us that the child did not know sign language.

We assumed that she was around third or fourth grade, but Mrs. Feldman said that she was a 12-year-old fifth grader. We were pretty surprised to learn that she was in the fifth grade. Her social interactions were closer to that of a second grader. When she had visited the classroom, she had flailed her arms, yelled out inappropriately, and made cartoon sounds with her voice. This typical second grade behavior was incongruous with her age.

I did not think much about it as I started my day. The students filed in one-by-one.

As the day progressed, a steady stream of the students' batteries went dead. We met at the table where the spare equipment was kept.

I asked Joey, "Which pack belongs to you?"

Joey spoke rapidly and I could not read his lips. I stopped him and asked him to sign.

"Oh, we do not have our own batteries," he signed in perfect SEE 2. "The school gives them to us. I think mine are in here," he said, pointing to a drawer.

Confused by this, I asked Mrs. Feldman to explain. She said that the batteries were provided by the AEA so that the parents did not have to buy them.

Interesting … providing free batteries ensured that the students remained aurally dependent, which is an incentive for them to wear hearing aids. If a student from poorer background could not afford new batteries, no problem; there were more at the school.

Hearing aids are great for certain things, but they interfere with a child's ability to focus with learning in a classroom setting. Deaf children have a problem with reading and listening simultaneously, because they are constantly looking around for the source of the sound. They do this because most are unable to discern specific sounds.

We changed out the students' batteries and went back to their class instruction.

Thursday, September 29

After a few days with Nathalie in our classroom, she and Emma's friendship began to click. This was good socially, but they would not stop mimicking each other. Whatever Emma did, Nathalie imitated. It became clear why Mrs. Feldman did not want us to emphasize our use of signs. Everything that anyone did, Nathalie parroted, from blowing our noses to running our fingers through our hair.

That meant two Emmas. "Not good," I thought.

Nathalie's mother had never known about any of the mainstream programs, including the interpreter services, the D/HH program, the AEA itinerant caseworkers, audiologists, speech therapists or teachers for the deaf.

In August, Nathalie's mother complained to the school-based speech therapist about her daughter's failing academic performance. She had been considering home schooling Nathalie.

"Didn't you know that we have a Deaf and Hard of Hearing program at Knight School?" The speech therapist replied.

Nathalie's mother had been floored by this new information. She felt that the information had been withheld just because Nathalie's speech skills were pretty close to that of a hearing child.

Nathalie read at a first-grade level. She did not know any signed words. She jumped out of her seat doing the pump fist dance, "Yea! Woo hoo!" whenever she got a *single* math problem correct.

It was obvious that Nathalie's former teachers did not clearly communicate their classroom expectations to her, thus reinforcing her inappropriate behaviors. But it was entirely the AEA's fault.

Mrs. Feldman believed Nathalie's mother should take the AEA to court for punitive damages.

She pointed to Nathalie and mutely signed, "She is that way because of them! The AEA!"

For the first time in a long time, I agreed with her.

182

Monday, October 3

A few days earlier, Mrs. Feldman and Mrs. Diaz had agreed that the accommodations for Toby's reading and writing would soon have to be revised because Toby misplaces his hearing aids/tele-loop all the time. So, it was decided that when Mrs. Diaz picked the topic out of the basket each morning, she would write it out on the overhead for Toby to read, instead. However, Toby's bigger problem was that he could *not* read…

Apparently in spite of broken listening devices, Toby's loss of being able to hear *them* was far more important to the school administrators than the fact that he was an illiterate child. They didn't factor in that, if/once Toby went completely deaf, his means of communicating with hearing people would remain severely compromised. Twisted priorities.

Emma was out sick, so Cassie asked me to help her develop her signing skills. She was practicing to take the exam to become certified by the Registry of Interpreters for the Deaf (RID). I stayed behind to provide constructive feedback to her.

Cassie and I went to the gym. The gym teacher had all of the students face him with their backs to the door. The gym teacher was at the far end of the gym, demonstrating the rules of the game while Cassie and I faced the students. Cassie began interpreting while I observed her. I suggested that she stand closer to the gym teacher, but she refused, saying that if she moved around all the time, the students would lose focus on her.

This was more of an excuse than a legitimate reason; Cassie was somewhat corpulent. She should have stayed closer to the gym teacher so that the students could choose to either watch her interpret or to read the gym teacher's lips.

After several minutes into the gym teacher's session, Kallie came upstairs from the art room to use the bathroom. She stopped at the door and began to tease Cassie. Kallie was wearing a form fitting blouse with a V shaped neckline. She quickly glanced across the room and then pulled up her shirt exposing her belly button. Cassie was unmoved, so she repeated the action, only this time, she stuck out her pierced tongue in the process.

Cassie continued her work without being distracted by Kallie's bothersome antics, but I was offended. This was a place where students get their education, not some bar where girls go wild.

Subtly, I hinted to Kallie to stop and let Cassie do her job. Kallie continued to tease Cassie relentlessly for several more seconds. Then I realized this could be a test of Cassie's perseverance for her upcoming RID exam. This was a good distraction test I thought. I noticed Kallie scanning the hallways.

I wondered what she was up to.

Kallie quickly pulled down the top of her V neck tee shirt and exposed to Cassie her bra. In an instant, she pulled up her shirt and galloped off to the bathroom.

I shot a look at Cassie to observe her facial expression. She was as equally horrified as I was; she clumsily paused and then got back to the interpreting task.

During my break, I finished typing my unfinished resignation letter, just in case...

Thursday, October 6

The PTA was having a fundraising ice cream event at a local hang-out, so I bought enough tickets for me and my family and tucked them away before starting my day.

Still disturbed by the bra exposing incident, I discussed it with Cassie. She suggested that I tell Mrs. Feldman. I felt intimidated by that idea. Kallie acted like a street savvy chick and was quite good at talking her way out of trouble. This was not a battle that I thought I could win.

In Mrs. Feldman's classroom, Emma had taken an early nap, so I stuffed flyers for the ice cream social into the student's take-home folders. I had specifically asked Kallie if she was going to be there, and I was relieved when she said no.

I was waiting for Emma to wake up from her nap when Cassie walked into the room with Alyssa. Confused, I asked Cassie why Alyssa was here.

"Mrs. Taylor's class is too hard for her. She is here to catch up with our help."

Alyssa sat down with Mrs. Feldman, and they reviewed the morning's lessons.

I continued questioning Cassie, "Why can't Toby and Emma stay in here all day, instead of going to the hearing classroom? It's not fair to them if she constantly helps one child all the time."

Cassie cautiously looked at Mrs. Feldman, who was oblivious to our conversation.

"She cannot handle all the deaf students at once, which is why she sends them out of the classroom whenever she can! And, the school policy requires the deaf students to become mainstreamed at some point."

I was irate, but I shook the feeling and woke Emma from her nap. Just as I did, Emma formed her hand to make a mock gun and pretended to shoot me with it, making cartoon sounds of gunfire as she did.

Emma was generally predictable but I needed her parents' help and involvement with reinforcing the disciplinary measures in this specific area.

A month earlier, being a farm girl herself, Emma had received a new BB gun for her birthday. Would she actually bring the BB gun to school and shoot me with it? Historically, Emma had brought foreign and strange objects to school in her backpack.

Mrs. Feldman immediately walked over to my side and told Emma to go to the principal's office. She assured me that everything was fine, but changed her mind when I told her, "I'm really concerned. Emma is now bigger than I am."

"I know," she said.

Mrs. Feldman told Cassie to watch the class while she and I went downstairs to the principal's office. The principal asked for my side of the story. Being new to the school, he was blown away by the fact that Emma had been getting away with this. He assured me that he would improve the system.

I had heard that before.

His assurance did not encourage me very much, especially when his solution was to send Emma home with a note explaining to her parents why she had been sent to the office. Her parents were supposed to read, sign and return the note. Right idea, but her parents are something else…

That night at the ice cream hang out, I found Mrs. Feldman and told her about Kallie exposing her bra while the students were in gym class. Mrs. Feldman was aghast. She suggested that I go directly to the principal or the school counselor about it.

So I did, but first…

Aware that Kallie would not take it lightly if I went to the principal about the incident, I decided it would be best to gather my allies; after the event, I went home and emailed a few people about what had happened. Had I felt that my job was secure, I would have reported it immediately to the principal in the first place. It was unfortunate that I had to rely on others like that.

Friday, October 7

I quickly dumped the contents of Emma's backpack looking for the signed paper. It was nowhere to be found.

"Emma, where is the principal's paper that your parents signed?"

"Home," she said as if she'd never been punished for it.

I was unsure if she understood the consequences of her actions, so I rephrased the question. "Did your parents read the paper?"

"Yes," she said, munching on one of the strange items from her backpack.

"Where is the BB gun now?" I asked.

"Top refrigerator," she said, still chewing on the foreign object.

"So you cannot use it for a week, right?" I probed deeper.

"No, me not punished. Mom Dad let me have it."

Emma, slowly and calculatedly, raised her right hand to her mouth, pointed at me with her left hand, and let out a slow, comical laugh, "Mu...ha...ha...ha..."

I was upset that Emma's parents were not being proactive with disciplinary measure to help us make the situation at school work. In essence, they were telling Emma that it was okay to threaten and even to hurt us.

A tap on my shoulder startled me. It was Kallie. She made herself comfortable, plopping down in the chair next to mine.

"I bet they'll change your schedule within two weeks. You'll be full-time by then. Emma's behavior is worse in the afternoons when you are not around, especially on Fridays with the mentoring program in the kindergarten."

Rather surprised that no one had told me about Emma's behavior in the kindergarten room.

"What can I do?" I shrugged.

As the end of my shift approached, I got up to get ready to leave. Mrs. Feldman asked me to help Emma at 2:30 in the kindergarten classroom.

I shook my head no. "I don't work after 12:30," I apologized disingenuously.

Mrs. Feldman sighed heavily and explained that the fourth and fifth graders are the kindergartner's mentors. The older students visit the kindergarteners every Friday for 15 to 30 minutes to establish a positive rapport with the younger students.

According to Kallie and Mrs. Feldman, Emma was at her worst during this time. Kallie usually had to take Emma out of the classroom, leaving the deaf students without an interpreter.

Some things never changed.

Tuesday, October 11

Mrs. Diaz's fourth grade class filed into the gym and sat on the floor. The gym teacher started with the roll call, and Kallie translated.

"He's calling out names — roll call."

After a few names were called out, Kallie looked at me and complained, "Shit! My fingers hurt from spelling out all of these names. I don't want to sign all of their names if they are not even watching me."

Disgustedly, she pointed at the deaf students. They were not watching the teacher or the interpreter. An awkward moment of silence followed, but as uncomfortable as I was, I did not know what to say to break it.

"Oh well," Kallie continued, "Wanna talk about my boobs?"

She laughed and then signed, "I thought I would wear this shirt so that your blind would not be hurt."

My mind raced, trying to figure out what she meant. Then I realized she intended to sign the word 'eyes' not 'blind'.

Kallie's shirt was the central point of her sarcasm. It was in bold swirled patterns with contrasting colors. This is not the type of shirt that interpreters should be wearing. That kind of pattern and color makes it difficult to watch the interpreter's hands. The shirt an interpreter wears is the backdrop of fast moving hands.

Kallie was an unskilled interpreter, working with deaf elementary students who had deficient literacy skills. Just when I thought I'd seen it all…

While the students were on the court playing games, I thought about three comments from an interpreter about Mrs. Feldman. The interpreter's main complaint was that Mrs. Feldman tried to integrate the deaf students because she did not want to deal with them; especially Emma. Mrs. Feldman tried her best to keep the deaf students in the hearing classrooms all day, except for Emma, who had to be kept in the deaf classroom part of the day. Perhaps Mrs. Feldman did not want to admit that the deaf students were not doing well in either classrooms — the hearing or the deaf.

After the gym lesson, we returned to Mrs. Feldman's classroom. Emma took a nap, so I assisted Dalton with his spelling words. After he had a few words and definitions penned, Dalton cocked his head, looked at me and said that Knight was the best school; better than the one he went to out of state.

"Why?" I asked him.

He looked left and right trying to find the right signs to express his idea. He slowly signed, explaining that the deaf students at the other school did not know any sign language. They moved their mouths too much — he mimicked their mouth movements like a fish gasping for water. He said that most of them had CIs.

"…and they do not understand me most of the time," he signed.

"Is it because you signed?" I asked.

"They didn't understand anyone else either. The talkers," Dalton replied.

In spite of his previous outbursts, it was good to have him back.

I recalled what one of the interpreters had told me about how his parents disciplined him. His father, who did not know sign language, turned into a drill sergeant when Dalton's behavior was unacceptable. He thought that by yelling and acting, Dalton would understand the point.

Friday, October 14

The deaf students took their spelling tests first thing every Friday. After helping them practice and memorize the words all week, I felt confident that most of them would do well.

There were three trapezoid tables that could seat two or three students each, where the deaf students sat so they could see each other. The rest of the students sat at desks while taking their spelling test.

As usual, I sat behind Emma at her trapezoid table while she took her spelling test. I could see Dalton becoming obviously agitated trying to recall the spelling words.

After the spelling test, I looked at Dalton's paper. Something was amiss. Mrs. Feldman had obstinately used SEE 1 while proctoring the spelling test, and she consistently misspelled the words.

For instance, she signed the words 'All' + 'So' for the word 'also', so nearly all of the deaf students wrote 'aso'. Mrs. Feldman clearly spoke and signed the two words 'Be' + 'Low' for the word 'below'. Again, none of the deaf students got it right. Dalton wrote 'buluo' on his paper.

After the test, we lined up the students and took them to the music room. On the way down, in ASL, I asked Dalton, to spell "below", and he got it down correctly. As mystified as I was, I moved on.

Obviously, the SEE 2 concept was not working, because all of the words were either being mis-signed or misspelled even in specific SEE morphemes. It was failing the students and the teachers.

In the music room, Emma gave the microphone to the teacher. As usual, she placed the device someplace other than near her mouth. The music teacher explained to the class what they were to do by acting as a conductor. The students were to pretend that they were in a band — acting and role playing. After a few practice stanzas, a female hearing classmate was chosen to take over as the conductor.

The girl led the band for two minutes without a glitch. The music teacher told her to choose the next person to lead.

"Me!"

"Pick me!"

"I'm your friend!"

"Oh! Here!"

Everyone's hands shot up except Emma's.

The girl chose one of her best friends. The second girl also led the band without a glitch.

"Now you get to pick someone to lead," the music teacher told the girl.

The second girl looked thoughtfully around the classroom at everyone's waving hands. She spotted Emma sitting quietly looking shy. As she picked Emma, the music teacher's face turned as white as a ghost.

Her eyes widened and her jaw dropped, simply incredulous at the girl's unlikely choice.

This was completely unexpected. The girl came from a very wealthy family and always hung out with kids who had similar lifestyles. The music teacher, who was still stunned, wanted to make sure that what she saw was actually happening.

"Are you sure that Emma can handle it?" she asked the girl.

"Yeah, can I pick Emma?" The girl replied.

Hinting to the child that she should choose someone else, she overly emphasized, "Are you sure?"

Kallie sardonically rolled her eyes. Apprehensively, the music teacher kept her distance from Emma as Emma directed the band... flawlessly.

I beamed with pride for her. Even more proud was the girl who chose her. This was such a rare moment for Emma.

Monday, October 17

Over the course of this week, the deaf students began staying in Mrs. Feldman's room more and more in the mornings.

I asked Mrs. Feldman why they were not in their hearing classroom.

"Too hard for them," Mrs. Feldman replied. "They go in for one or two hours in the morning to write in their journals, then they come back here, and we help them with their assigned work. It's the same in the afternoons."

Imagine that... if nothing changes, nothing changes (same old, same old; same as it ever was). At least the students were learning something.

Kallie and I later escorted the students to the art room. There was a retired Knight teacher substituting for the regular art teacher. Kallie sat against the blackboard at the back of the room, and I sat with Emma at her assigned seat. Joey had his hand raised for quite some time. The substitute teacher approached Kallie:

"Joey needs you now. He's been waiting for you to help him."

The substitute walked off to continue teaching.

Kallie trotted over to the teacher and corrected her, "Answering the students' questions is your responsibility."

Visibly stressed, the substitute retorted, "Joey is your student. You are here to help."

She resumed teaching.

Joey has had his hand up for several minutes, so Kallie relented and went over to him.

"Yes, what is your question?" She asked.

Joey asked something about using the art supplies. Kallie shot a look at me and threw her arms up in the air. "I knew it! That question was for the teacher! I don't know anything in this classroom!" She vented.

The principal was called to resolve the conflict. He told the substitute that all the students were her responsibility. Interpreters were to remain within the scope of their duty, which was to interpret as long as the teacher was talking.

We returned from the art class to Mrs. Feldman's classroom, where the deaf students performed a fun exercise game.

The students were divided into two rows of equal numbers. The first person in the first row was to face the first person in the opposite row. The second person was to face the second person, and so on.

The game was called "Copy Face." This was a free-play game in which one person was to make a face and their partner was to copy it exactly. Each of the partners got to create their own facial expressions. They were on their own.

As usual, I stood behind Emma, shadowing her.

Just as Mrs. Feldman assigned the students to their rows, some of the students realized that they would be paired up with Emma and wildly scrambled to switch places, shoving each other out of the way.

Eventually, there was an empty seat across from Emma. The students became nervous, knowing that Mrs. Feldman would rearrange them so that Emma would have a partner.

Mrs. Feldman observed the students' placements and switched Toby and Dalton. Rachel wanted to stay with Alyssa, but Mrs. Feldman put Brendan with Alyssa and Rachel with Emma.

As soon as Mrs. Feldman released her grip from Rachel's shoulders, Rachel pouted, "I quit!"

Mrs. Feldman threatened to take Rachel's recess time, but the child was unmoved by Mrs. Feldman's threat. Rather surprised by Rachel's imperturbable confidence, I thought to myself, "This kid owns Mrs. Feldman!"

Rachel continued to be utterly rude to Emma.

Mrs. Feldman announced, "Let the game begin!"

Emma gestured for Rachel to participate, but Rachel moved further back, leaning on one of the desks, looking away. Mrs. Feldman immediately gave Rachel a nudge back toward the vacant spot. Rachel swung her arm, breaking free from Mrs. Feldman's grip. She stepped back even farther. Emma stood there making faces by herself.

"What you are doing is not team spirit!" Mrs. Feldman chastised Rachel.

Unperturbed, Rachel shrugged, looked away and stared out the window.

Mrs. Feldman waddled over to Emma and took Rachel's abandoned position. The game was saved.

Just as I was ready to leave for the day, I asked one of the interpreters if she thought that Mrs. Feldman would keep her promise about disciplining Rachel.

Cassie shook her head, "Never. She always lets them out."

Even a deaf girl, Rachel, knew that Emma was different. Stigma was associated with her, and the teachers did nothing to stop it. Just imagine what it was like for Emma on a daily basis — students refusing to sit with her in the cafeteria or to play with her during recess.

The Deaf kids playing and eating alone scenario has been the classic exemplification of a failed LRE mandate, and here it was happening even in the inclusive program's deaf classroom.

Tuesday, October 18

First thing in the morning, I asked Mrs. Feldman if she kept Rachel in during recess. With a guilty look on her face, she said that Rachel went out to play. That is why Rachel was unconcerned with Mrs. Feldman's threats; she never did anything to back them up. Rachel knew that Mrs. Feldman's words meant nothing.

Cassie watched our conversation and waited for Mrs. Feldman to leave the room before she came over.

Coffee in one hand, signing with the other, she said, "Mrs. Feldman's worst nightmare is having the students in the classroom, F-Y-I."

That morning, the deaf students were to take the National Standardized Testing (NST) assessment. Emma could not handle this particular task. She stabbed my hand with a sharpened pencil. She was sent to the principal's office for the rest of the day and was supposed to take the test there.

As it happened, Emma's mother was there dropping off a spare pair of eyeglasses. Alyssa also coincidentally showed up outside of the nurse's office in the hallway, waiting for a Band-Aid. I waited with Emma in the hallway next to the principal's office door.

In the office, the principal was discussing with Emma's mother about her daughter's stressors.

Out in the hallway, as Alyssa appeared, Emma haphazardly spotted her.

Then Emma's face and neck reddened as she yelled at the top of her lungs, "Alyssa! Moron!"

Still pointing at Alyssa, she finished off with a rhythmic taunting, "Alyssa! Baby baby baby baby..."

The school nurse quickly ushered Alyssa into her office and shut the door.

Not shocked at Emma's outburst, I closed all of the remaining doors in the hallway and waited with her until the principal and Emma's mother were finished with the meeting. She came out still clutching Emma's spare glasses. Emma's mother and I chatted. She was apologetic, but I reminded her that Emma had made great leaps and bounds. She was relieved, and then we hugged. Emma was turned over to them as I left work early. My hand was bleeding from being stabbed.

Friday, October 21

It was the last day of National Standardized Testing week.

The art teacher was showing pictures of art pieces in a big book that she had resting on an easel. She explained to the students that they had to memorize three answers from the bottom of the pages. Most of the deaf students could see the easel, except Joey. He swayed left and right, crouched lower and craned his neck trying to get a better view. Noticing this, I asked Kallie if she would step aside a little so that Joey could see the book.

"Interpreting is my job. Joey has to learn to use this service and rely on interpreters," Kallie answered.

"Well, I know, but at least let him choose whether to look at you or to look at the book. The hearing students can listen to the teacher and look at the book at the same time. Please let Joey have that equal option," I pled my case.

"No. If he can't see the easel, then he has to move to a better place. He has to learn to rely only on me."

The art teacher handed out assignments and the students were to answer questions using their memory.

When the students had completed the assignment, the teacher collected the papers and handed the deaf students' worksheets to me to correct. Most of the deaf students got it right — except Joey. His paper was riddled with errors.

Later, I asked Kallie, "Why did you do that, anyway? Joey was the only deaf kid who got every single answer wrong."

"His parents insist that I make him learn how to use interpreters. It's his responsibility to listen."

Still, that was inappropriate for this task.

Immediately after art class, Mrs. Feldman told me to work with Joey. She believed that she could make Emma take the NST.

"Be sure to have 100 pencils handy. She snaps each one in half. You'll be dishing out pencils in rapid succession," I tried to warn her.

"I'll handle this. She might feel more comfortable working with me because she knows you're stressed. She can sense it."

I was stressed all right, but it wasn't because of Emma. My patience was wearing thin with Mrs. Feldman's naiveté, so I set her straight.

"I am not stressed or frustrated. She is doing this because she does not want to take the test, period, and you all still won't let me or her favorite adult try to mark down her best picks."

Emma looked relieved.

I had never spoken so bluntly with Mrs. Feldman before, and she did not know quite how to respond. She changed her mind and ordered me to go to the teacher's desk to work with Emma, away from Joey.

Joey and Ms. Feldman went to the interpreter's desk and reviewed the directions on the NST. He started right away.

As Joey took his test, Ms. Feldman looked over his shoulder. She looked over at me. I was busy with Emma. Apparently, he was working on punctuation and had chosen the incorrect answer on one of the questions. She reminded Joey that sentences with who, where, when, what, why, and how, end with a question mark. Joey scanned his paper and found a few errors. He changed his answers and resumed taking the test. All of this took place at the edge of my peripheral vision.

Joey had a hard time concentrating on the test, because Emma was being as loud as one can be. She was screaming and pounding the table repetitively. She threw a box of pencils up in the air, and we all crouched, covering our eyes to protect them from being jabbed with the sharp pointy lead.

Immediately after throwing the pencils in the air, Emma willfully collapsed on the floor and took a nap right on the spot.

Monday, October 24

As we entered the music room, I instructed Emma to hand the music teacher the microphone. Emma grabbed the device from my hand and started singing in it, skipped a little toward the teacher and jerked her arm forward in a robotic fashion.

The music teacher carefully lifted the microphone from Emma's hand, and as she stepped backwards, she mumbled something. With a repulsed look on her face, she dropped the microphone onto her desk.

Kallie's eyes widened and she mutely signed, "Oh shit! I heard what she said! A few of them giggled because they heard it too."

Not knowing what she was talking about, I said, "What? Who said what?"

"When Emma gave the microphone to the music teacher, the teacher looked all grossed out and said very loudly, 'Eww gross! She had that in her mouth!' Can you imagine that? A grown adult thinks Emma is beneath her! That's disgusting!"

It was heartbreaking to see an adult behave this way.

The music teacher started a new lesson, and Kallie interpreted. Emma was complaining that she could not hear the teacher's voice over the students' singing.

"Tell her to use the microphone around her neck!" I demanded.

"I can't, I'm busy interpreting!" Kallie said defensively.

I waved at the music teacher, but she intentionally looked in the opposite direction. Kallie continued interpreting. Emma pinched me.

"Oww! Okay, you stay here and I will go upstairs and tell Mrs. Feldman why you can't hear the music teacher," I told Emma.

Emma nodded and gestured. "Microphone. All sing too loud," she complained. She was nearly in tears when I left the room.

I returned a few minutes later with Mrs. Feldman. She ordered the music teacher to put Emma's microphone around her neck.

197

The music teacher's face turned gray and the life went out of her eyes. She briefly glanced at me before resuming the lesson with Emma's microphone around her neck.

I felt uneasy for putting her in an awkward position, but a child's education is more important. Kallie was an interpreter *and* a teacher's aide. She should have relayed the important message to the music teacher — even if she was in the middle of interpreting for the deaf students.

I checked my email account during my break. There was a message from the principal. He had made an appointment with me, along with an interpreter certified by the RID. I had a sinking feeling that this was about Kallie having flashed Cassie and me in the gym.

Peering over the computer monitor, I asked Cassie, "Do you remember the bra flashing incident?"

Cassie covered her head with her hands and shook her head, "I don't remember anything," she replied, awkwardly looking away.

Shocked at her short-term memory, I said, "You don't remember? It happened only days ago!"

"I'm pregnant! Maybe that's why I don't remember."

Rather taken aback with this new revelation of her pregnancy, I reminisced over Angela's prophetic remark nearly two years before... I then realized who my friends really were. I left work wondering who would vouch for my complaint.

Tuesday, October 25

I sent Emma downstairs to the cafeteria to have her breakfast, but I changed my mind when I discovered that the music teacher had breakfast duty.

"Disaster," I thought.

I quickly scrambled downstairs, only to find the music teacher was shaking Emma's hand. Then she hugged her. I was elated that she was trying to overcome the feelings that she had toward Emma.

I looked at the clock. I did not want to be late for my meeting with the principal and a bunch of important people, so I went over to the principal's office.

Each of them took turns shaking my hand, offering a formal introduction.

"Why are we having this meeting? What is it about?"

The principal cut straight to the point. "We know what's been going on. Why don't you tell us about what happened on the morning when one of the interpreters pulled down her shirt? Why didn't you discuss the situation about Mrs. Smith when you were here observing her in 2002, when you saw her be rough with some of the students?"

I gave them my version of the story.

The union representative replied coldly, "Why didn't you immediately report all of this?"

From there on, they grilled me about my faults for not reporting the flashing incident right away and for not reporting what had happened in Mrs. Smith's class. It dawned to me that Mrs. Feldman didn't even report the incident on my behalf.

As the meeting ended, the principal said, "I'll talk to Kallie about it. She is not to harass you anymore."

Concerned about her attitude towards me, I asked, "How did you know it was her?"

The human resource manager spoke up and said, "She was referred to the office 8 times last year."

The principal looked surprised and said, "I didn't know that. Was that with the previous principal?"

The manager nodded.

Before the meeting was over, I asked the principal, "Is my job at risk?"

He shot an alarmed look at me and replied, "Everyone started a new slate with me. Kallie now has one marked down. Don't say anything at all to her. I've got this."

I asked the principal if he could switch interpreters in Mrs. Diaz's class.

"No. Things will remain the same as they were before. She is to respect you from now on. You can expect that," he said as he wagged his finger at me.

Suddenly, my stomach turned queasy, so I used my sick leave to go home. I had been taking a lot of sick days since working with Kallie. A thought of Joey appeared, and I recalled the day on the blacktop during recess when Joey revealed to me that he didn't even want Kallie to be his interpreter. Oh geez. Poor Joey.

Wednesday, October 26

My stomach flipped and flopped all night and through-out the morning. I loved my job with Emma, but this absurdity was wearing me out. I didn't know how much longer I might last.

I walked into Mrs. Feldman's classroom and headed for the desk. I put away my purse and my snack, and I turned to Emma's 'educational' needs.

Kallie appeared in the room and stole my gaze. She was seething with rage. The rhythm of her usual bouncing dance was missing; her customary two-handed hello was eerily absent.

I knew that she knew.

Three deaf students, Kallie and I walked into Mrs. Diaz's room.

Kallie stood next to Mrs. Diaz and conducted her duties as expected. She then announced that Mr. Bryant had a special skit for the class and that we were to immediately go in there and sit down.

Just as we got up to leave the room, Kallie grabbed Emma by the arm away from me and walked out into the hallway toward Mr. Bryant's classroom, leaving me stranded — without Emma, I lacked working tasks. It seemed she was determined to take away my job.

As quickly as I could walk, I caught up with Kallie and Emma. I grabbed a chair for Emma, but Kallie grabbed one also. Emma took the chair from Kallie, so I sat in the chair I was holding. All three of us sat in the back of the room, near the door.

Mrs. Diaz and Kallie sat on Emma's left and I sat on Emma's right.

Emma asked me to explain what the skit was about. Kallie was chatting with Mrs. Diaz, so I got up to interpret for Emma. Kallie ordered me to stop and to sit down because microphones had been strategically placed near the actors. Emma still objected and became cranky.

"Sleep please, me tired." She plaintively moaned.

I waved into Mrs. Diaz's line of vision and gestured Emma's message. Kallie interrupted me:

"She does not know sign language!"

A bit taken aback by her tone, I explained myself, "No, I was telling her that Emma wanted to be excused for her nap — that's all, and she needs an interpreter."

"Still…" Kallie said, shrugging her shoulders. She fidgeted her hands, searching for one last comeback — and she found it:

"Mrs. Diaz does not know sign language!" She said, brushing me off.

That was it. I knew that I couldn't take this anymore, especially with Kallie barking at me like that. Right on the spot, it was over.

Feeling crushed, I made my way to Mrs. Feldman's room to gather my things.

"Mrs. Feldman?" I whispered.

Looking up from where she was sitting at the trapezoid table she said, "Yes?"

"I'm leaving now. Goodbye." I said, and I left the room.

Mrs. Feldman quickly caught up with me in the hallway. Standing near Mr. Bryant's classroom, the deaf students' eyes and mine locked. They were watching us.

"Oh, how awkward," I thought to myself.

Kallie hadn't noticed that they weren't paying attention to the skit because she was busy chatting with Mrs. Diaz.

Mrs. Feldman asked me why I was leaving.

"None of you would switch interpreters!" The students were still watching us, so I turned my back to the students.

Looking at Mrs. Feldman once again, I reduced my spatial signs. I told her my perspective about the incorrectly applied SEE 2 method, missing or broken assistive devices, interpreters not doing their jobs, numerous IEP violations, and zero input environments. I told her flashbacks about phonetic assignments and crying deaf students.

Perturbed, I signed, "…and none of you would listen!"

After all of this, she still thought I could get through the day. She didn't take me seriously or give my point of view a valid thought.

The deaf students were still looking at us by the time I turned to leave. I smiled and waved at them, then signed, "Crazy, huh?"

All but Dalton waved back animatedly. Dalton shot up from his seat grinning, and he signed, "They crazy." Alyssa pointed at Dalton and started to giggle. Emma was on the hard linoleum floor, fast asleep. Smiling sadly, I left her there.

I handed in my resignation letter to the secretary and the principal. They asked me to show up for a farewell party during the staff breakfast in the library that Friday.

They did not ask me any questions, nor did they offer me any solutions, just as it had been for a lot of the deaf students. I gladly skipped out on my own farewell party.

While I may have felt defeated by the inclusion program at Knight School, the deaf children were the real casualties. They were trapped by educational mandates, caught in unethical situations created by the LRE madness.

"Kindness is a language which the deaf
can hear and the blind can see."

Mark Twain

EPILOGUE

Among many of today's school administrators, educators, parents, and case managers, possible communication methods (ASL, SEE 2, lip-reading, speech) are weighed against the D/HH students' ability to speak. Their intentions are in no way malicious, but only to help deaf and hard-of-hearing children become active members of society, while avoiding significant changes in the cultural and linguistic aspects of the school district's educational methods. However, the LRE mandate and the IEP process still do not resolve the particular issues I encountered. Schools are still not addressing the fact that D/HH students are not having their educational and social needs met.

The monetary and ethical issues of the LRE mandate could be simplified if a few things were honestly addressed. Hopefully, the scenarios discussed in this book shed new light on education for everyone involved. These experiences are no stranger to many deaf children, who are the byproduct of the LRE mandate. From a cultural and linguistic perspective, there is a common ground in education, and the deaf community is waiting to be heard. Here are possible solutions to these problems:

Hire certified Deaf, hard-of-hearing, or late deafened (LD) teachers and/or D/HH/LD teacher aides, so the D/HH students may have a role model.

Hire a Head Interpreter, the same way schools hire Department Heads, to provide refresher sign language courses, update work ethics, resolve conflicts, arrange rotational duties to prevent unhealthy alliances from forming, provide one-on-one consultations, and possibly act as a substitute interpreter if hearing.

Hire a culturally Deaf or entirely Deaf specialist to work in the Area Education Agency (AEA). Hearing parents will be inspired for their deaf child's future by meeting with a specialist who happens to be a deaf person. There is a probability that a deaf specialist would prevent the AEA from withholding educational options, such as in Nathalie's case where her parents were not informed about the mainstreamed program. This designated Deaf AEA specialist should be present at all IEP meetings for deaf students and deaf parents.

School districts need to reexamine their IEP consultation protocol. The entirety of school administrators and staff should be required to understand and be able to explain the options to parents. Parents should know before starting the IEP meeting that support services, such as listening assistive devices and speech therapy, are optional. The school staff should respect culturally Deaf parents' wishes that their culturally Deaf child not be required to wear listening assistive devices and/or attend speech therapy sessions. Parents often do not realize that an IEP is a contract between educators, parents, and students and that educators are *public employees* who should respect the parents' reasonable wishes without qualms.

States need to be brought up to speed and require a sign language license or certification for all "signers" - special-ed teachers, interpreters, and support staff that work directly with D/HH students. This should be done solely for the equal educational access required in IEPs, just as language arts teachers are required to have English Language Learners certification if they work with students of other linguistic backgrounds. This D/HH requirement should include teachers of the special-related classes, subjects in which D/HH students have specific needs different than hearing students. In doing this, the IEP team will be able to make appropriate educational placements for D/HH students, satisfying their communication needs through the hiring of qualified and/or certified "signers."

In any student, isolation creates problems in self-identity, self-esteem, and socialization skills. Reciprocal socialization plays a major role in developing socio-cognitive areas, therefore it is essential to keep D/HH students together based on their age and level, enabling a critical mass of social equals. The behavioral cues of students, deaf or hearing, are one of the indicators of whether an educational program, especially regarding the social and communication aspects, is a success or a failure. This concept applies to the home life as well as the school life.

In all that's been said, it is clear Deaf schools are an ideal place to acquire language and to preserve deaf culture. And the right thing to do is to keep Deaf schools open as it is ideally the "least restrictive environment" for deaf students, a home-away-from-home.

Conclusively, the Least Restrictive Environment of most schools does not offer these equal educational opportunities for the deaf and hard-of-hearing students. Full visual and sign language access is essential for equal educational opportunity access. Perhaps, if the Deaf culture and linguistic differences were brought to surface and were taken seriously within the education setting, our tax dollars could be put to better use. We could have solutions and successes rather than victims and failures. The deaf children educated under the LRE mandate no longer would be associated with the generalized perception of being *Deaf Beneath.*

Most of the students in this book have graduated, and while I think about them often, I was not able to follow their progress. But who could forget Emma? Emma never met a person she didn't like, despite her misbehavior. Emma's home school district finally agreed to meet her educational needs by the time she went into 8th grade. She had a one-on-one educational aide until she graduated from high school, and she was allowed to have a space where she could decompress with the school counselor as she did her assignments, anytime during school hours. Shortly after her graduation, she passed away in her sleep from long term health complications, and she was surrounded by her brothers, her family members and her pets. She will be missed dearly by all.

As for Knight School, the inclusive program is still limping along. Mrs. Smith has transferred out of state and continues to work as a D/HH teacher. Mrs. Jones retired shortly after my departure. Mrs. Feldman continues to teach but in a different school district. Mrs. Miller is now a teacher at a private school. Interpreters frequently come and go to different schools, and their whereabouts are unknown. And I, after obtaining my Master of Science degree in Education, I am still working within the system, trying to bring awareness to educators and to families. I keep in touch with friends made during this three-year experience, but we all see change coming slowly or not at all.

I hope that the problems illustrated by the scenarios in this book demonstrate to all of those who are strong proponents of implementing, evolving and perfecting the LRE mandate the work which must still be done to accomplish that goal. I hope this call for change reaches all those who need to see examples of this nearly unspoken and literally rarely heard side of education. I hope reading this book changes the hearts and minds of those who have the power to make a difference in education. If you are a lawmaker or an administrator, I hope these examples touch you. If you are a parent with a child still in school, I hope they enlighten you. If you care about the future of children in America, then I hope the plight of the children whose lives are detailed in this book reaches out to you. If we all act on the aforementioned issues proactively and efficiently, we shall see a huge improvement in overcoming these literacy crises among Deaf students within a generation or two.

APPENDIX

This section offers a brief overview of the Americans with Disabilities Act, special education funding, and descriptions and functions of commonly used words in deaf education programs.

Since the inception of the Americans with Disabilities Act (ADA) in 1993, the deaf education program has experienced a shortage of interpreters and a shortage of qualified educators of deaf and hard of hearing students, as well as an increase in the number of incompetent interpreters and educators of deaf students. ADA has also propelled cochlear implantation programs, which have grown exponentially and indirectly are the cause of an influx of students with hearing loss in the mainstream programs. ADA also indirectly affected the closure of many residential state schools for the deaf, affectionately known as 'Deaf Schools.'

Special education funding issues in regards to the closure of Deaf Schools.

Public school systems generally do not have the money to support extraneous faculty exclusively for the culturally deaf students who use American Sign Language (ASL); the ratio is against their favor. On the grounds of budgetary limitations, it saves the state some money to send the deaf students to wherever there is stronger language support, when there is a school already established, rather than providing local support. One such school would be the Deaf School, which serves only Deaf/Hard of Hearing students. The state saves even more money if the district lumps all students of the same grade level into one classroom and provides just one interpreter per grade where possible. In other words, the lower functioning deaf student with multi-disabilities would be in the same class as the academically achieving deaf student, as it is with some of the situations in this book.

Due to critical funding issues, there have been many who considered simply closing schools that exclusively service the deaf community. This would mean that many deaf students would have to attend their local public school. However, in a meeting regarding the

207

possible closing of the Ohio School for the Deaf and Ohio State School for the Blind, it was pointed out that the services provided by these schools do not directly cost the local school district or the parent. They are funded entirely by state and federal funds.

Whether these changes are viable or impossible in their budget projections is determined according to the number of deaf students that attend a school district that has a one hundred percent inclusive program for deaf students. When these deaf students are re-integrated into the regular classroom setting, it can cost the district upwards of $100,000 to provide the services necessary for the education of a *single* student. (Ohio State School for the Deaf, 2007). With the closure of Deaf Schools, the burden would be shifted from the state and federal agencies to the local school district and the local community through increased taxes.

These expenses are a real cost associated with the closure of the Deaf schools. However, it is clear that these real costs are not being considered in the decision to close the Deaf schools. Those that are in favor of closing these Deaf schools only consider the costs of *operation* of the school that is being closed. They do not consider the additional expense to the local school district and community. They are only looking at one side of the budgetary issues, rather than looking at the total spending picture. This is a shortsighted approach that will cost more in the long-term. The *negative* "opportunity costs" are ignored.

Additionally, most discussions on the issue have remained focused exclusively on budgetary limitations, with little discussion of the consequences for the deaf students. Although many of the deaf students can successfully integrate into the local school setting, it is not without great expense and effort on everyone's part. Plenty of educational approaches for deaf students have been tried. However, if the priority is preserving their deaf culture, one has to consider what is best for the deaf community rather than for the majority of Americans. Although seeming to promote more isolation in general settings, embracing "deaf culture" allows the students to more fully develop their ability to express them selves and to reach their optimum potential communication levels as self sufficient, dignified human beings – without limiting them to the burdens and restrictions of dealing verbally, however poorly, with hearing people.

This book was written in the hopes that school administrators, educators and parents would reflect on their educational approach and improve the teaching method for deaf students. It is a way of producing detailed insights (such as those from observations) that can be used to solve specific predicaments. Perhaps this book will be able to offer some assistance to the administrators of deaf education programs who are willing to look more closely at the problematic areas.

However, as we seek the answers to these questions, we must not forget to include the student as a major stakeholder in these decisions. There are ways to resolve budgetary issues and still provide the student with the optimal learning environment. It will take cooperation between all parties involved. Perhaps the most important factor is to always remember to place students as the first priority.

The following labels are assigned to shorten and clarify descriptions of deafness, as stated below.

The mainstreamed programs for the deaf and hard of hearing students are abbreviated from deaf and hard of hearing to D/HH for D/HH programs and D/HH individuals.

Throughout in this paper, the tone is set based on separating the definitions of people with deafness and people with strong deaf identity. Deafness is separated into small 'd' as deaf and alternatively to big 'D' as Deaf. The rationale for the differences is that the small 'd' refers to the physical condition of deafness and also to deaf people who lack Deaf identity through their choices of socialization and mode of communication. A deaf-mute also cannot verbalize. The big 'D' refers to people with close ties with the Deaf community, and the mode of communication they favor is to use American Sign Language. As far as Deaf community goes, it is defined in generalized terms as the cultural norms established and accepted by the community of Deaf individuals. All of these deaf and Deaf terms will be used interchangeably.

What is IDEA?

The Individuals with Disabilities Education Act (IDEA) was adapted in 1975 from the Education for All Handicapped Children Act (PL 94-142). Amended in 2004 to the Individuals with Disabilities Education Improvement Act, it enables parents to play active roles in making educational decisions for their children with special-needs. This kind of parental involvement is called an Individualized Educational Plan (IEP).

Before the IDEA, people thought Least Restrictive Environment (LRE) meant putting a deaf child into a mainstreamed environment close to home, thereby making it equally accessible, just as hearing children receive education close to home. However, they did not factor in the potential socio-psychological impact it would have on a deaf child, especially when there is not much deaf peer interaction. This idea came from the Russian philosopher and educational psychologist, Lev Vygotsky. He argued strongly for peer interaction as necessary to build up social intelligence. Essentially, to a deaf child, the most favorable Least Restrictive Environment would be at the Deaf school.

A tip for primary caretakers: IDEA favors the whole placement of a child, rather than the educational aspect for the child alone. To maximize deaf childrens' education, apply the law section 504 and register ASL as the students' primary language on the IEP. This clause will force the school to hire certified and educated ASL interpreters.

What is LRE?

The LRE mandate is a spin-off from IDEA, as discussed in the above section. The LRE is characterized as the educational mandate where a child with a disability must receive a free and appropriate education. The education is designed to meet his or her educational needs while being educated with peers without disabilities in the regular educational environment to the maximum extent *appropriate*.

Mainstreaming was the precept behind PL 94-142, which was a legislation pushed through by congress in order to allow students with disability to be educated alongside their non-disabled peers. Unfortunately, Deaf people were lumped together under the disability category and were forced to go to schools where their communication needs were not met.

Public schools still face problems associated with the LRE mandate. Deaf education in public schools has two main aspects:

1. Least Restrictive Environment (Inclusive)

2. Individualized Education Plan (Support Service)

As D/HH students move through these two aspects, their educational access becomes unequal. There is very little evidence that shows deaf and hard of hearing students actually succeed on the same level as their hearing counterparts. This is true whether the D/HH students are mainstreamed or the D/HH students are kept in special education classrooms most of the day.

The National Association for the Deaf (NAD) disagreed with the LRE mandate, claiming that it is greatly misunderstood and misused in deaf education. It is intriguing that the supporters of LRE view the deaf education in public schools as equal, while the views of the majority of the Deaf community are just the opposite.

What is an IEP?

An Individual Education Plan is a community agreement between parents and educational team members to ensure the child with disability receives a fair and appropriate education in order to educationally strive. For instance, in the community meeting between the parents and the educational team members, they may agree that the deaf child will receive interpreter services, note taking services, the use of aural systems, and other support services available.

Each deaf student receives individualized educational attention in order to receive as equal an access to education as his or her hearing peers. Not all individualized attention is created equal. One deaf student may not need an interpreter service, while another deaf student may need more than just one supplemental assistance.

Isolating the deaf child in a hearing classroom away from their deaf peers is often erroneously regarded as the "Least Restrictive Environment." The IEP process is supposed to reinforce the LRE mandate and vice versa. However, the actual effect of mainstreaming deaf children in a class is that they sit alone without peer interaction from hearing students. And it is the very professionals devoted to remedying the social problems attending deafness who continue to promote this incorrect claim concerning the LRE.

What is a support service?

A support service is also called a support team, team member, intervention service, intervention team, rehabilitative service, rehabilitative team, etc. The Area Education Agency (or so-called AEA is often mirrored under different acronyms elsewhere, under the special education departments) provides a support service consisting of a wide range of itinerant team members and therapists, such as speech therapists, audiologists, language development therapists, physical therapists, occupational therapists, special-ed teachers, counselors, and nurses. Some cases involve private support services provided by the student's health insurance.

What is the aural system?

The aural system is commonly used in the D/HH classroom. D/HH individuals can have a range of hearing loss, from no hearing from birth, to partial hearing loss or tone deafness. This system is designed to maximize the development of spoken and listening skills.

Aural systems consist of sound amplification systems, such as the personal frequency modulation (FM) system equipped with a personal microphone for the teacher, induction loop (tele-loop), listening devices, and other listening aids for deaf students. The aural devices provided by the school are to enable deaf students to hear the teacher's voice through the assigned microphone.

There are special considerations regarding aural systems in classrooms. Without FM trainers, the D/HH students have difficulty keeping their eyes on the teacher because they may keep hearing external noises other than the teacher's speech. On the other hand, fiddling with FM trainers to ensure that they work can cause students to lose valuable academic time.

What is SEE 1?

David Anthony created Seeing Essential English (SEE 1) in 1966. One of the key requirements of using SEE 1 is applying a signed word for each recognizable word shape in a compound word, which may or may not be correct morphemic parts. All compound words have their own signed corollaries. For instance, the compound word of 'belong' (verb) would be split into two signed words, 'be' (verb) and 'long' (adjective) in this sequential order. This type of syntactic approach is linguistically illogical, therefore unacceptable.

What is SEE 2?

Gerilee Gustason created Signing Exact English 2 (SEE 2) in 1972. SEE 2 is an offshoot of Anthony's creation of SEE 1. SEE 2 is widely used in deaf education programs because it provides a grammatically structured language. The compound words are not separated into their own signed words. SEE 2 has signed words for affixes, past, present, and future tenses. One of the key requirements of using SEE 2 in mainstream deaf education program is using speech, either simultaneous communication (SimCom) or Signed-Support Speech.

However, the improper use of signs is not the only problem. SEE signers also use signs for people's ethnicity now considered politically incorrect. For example, SEE 2 uses the "C" hand shape next to the eye to indicate 'Chinese,' instead of the more appropriate sign for the word based on the hefu, their traditional clothing. The SEE signs may be offensive to ethnic individuals, and they confuse deaf children who are just beginning to learn sign.

This type of syntactic approach is also linguistically illogical for education because a word with multiple meanings with different definitions shares the same signed method. For instance, the multiple meaning word *can* in its verb sense or its noun sense has only one signed word, which is assigned to all the multiple meanings.

SEE 2 signers often switch to SEE 1 without realizing it, because they have been signing this way for so long. There is usually no one to rectify this problem.

Throughout this book, SEE 1 and SEE 2 will be referred to as SEE, or otherwise specified.

What is ASL?

American Sign Language has its own grammar and syntax. This is the only language that provides three-dimensional communication, pronoun spatiality, and manages to demonstrate outlined and iconic images. The use of speech is not existent in ASL.

213

Conceptually, some words like *can* have their own signs. The verb sign of *can* and the noun sign of *can* are signed differently according to their meanings, and this is done in order to match the grammar and syntactic approach. This approach is linguistically logical; therefore, it should be accepted and used in the public school system.

The natural language for deaf students is ASL; therefore, it makes sense that educational institutions would adopt practices that promote ASL education for deaf and hard of hearing students. However, American public schools have used English as the language of instruction to the virtual exclusion of other languages, including when teachers have low perceptions of deaf students' abilities to use ASL. It is vital that deaf students are provided opportunities for full knowledge and usage of ASL and the opportunity to work with educators who are fully trained in ASL. This may help raise academic expectations and achievement for students.

The Deaf community considers American Sign Language the standard language for culturally Deaf individuals. However, SEE 2 has penetrated into deaf education with more force than ASL, and many experts argue the potential merits and disadvantages of using one versus another in an educational and communicational context.

Linguist William Stokoe recognized that ASL is a fully developed language with unique grammar requirements distinguished from the English language. The Deaf community regards Stokoe as a hero based on his recognition of a language that has been oppressed by the majority of the hearing community.

Deaf people who use ASL exclusively are a linguistic minority, and they don't consider themselves disabled.

Source: Ohio School for the Deaf / Ohio State School for the Blind (2007). New Building Project Advisory Committee Meeting Minutes.

Ohio School for the Deaf Conference Center. August 14-15, 2007. Retrieved October 25, 2007 from www (dot) newcampus (dot) ossb (dot) oh (dot) gov/documents/advisorycommitteeminutes070820 (dot) pdf

About the Author

Libby Lael spent her early years in a University Speech and Hearing clinic, where she and her deaf sister were fitted with body-suspended hearing aid device and were made to attend audistic speech sessions. To this day, she is an oral failure, who chooses to stay mute under certain circumstances and who does not wear any hearing assistive devices.

With no end to literacy problems in sight for deaf people, and to circumvent the audistic environment, she chooses to use her UbiDuo2, a two-way face-to-face communication device, almost exclusively – as her main means of communicating with hearing people and non-signers. Text based communication is an excellent approach for deaf people to learn reading and writing, and to work/communicate with hearing people. Looking back at her educational upbringing, she now finds she would have liked to have had greater communication options and access, especially to digital communication.

Since the release of *Deaf Beneath*, she has switched her line of focus from an in-person educational setting to a more remote digital engagement.

With absolutely no background and experience in graphic design, her only resource on hand was Microsoft Word.doc. She used that resource to design several more book covers for her mentor, Herb Borkland. In addition to Libby's first project, for Herb Borkland's *DOG$*, helped make his novel a hot-seller in Europe, her latest book covers and custom layouts can be seen on his recent two books – *A Crime Not To Try* and *A Borkland Variety.*

A creative hobby which she stumbled upon by a stroke of luck in which she enjoys immensely. Currently, she is digitally assisting others. In her free time, she enjoys conversing with hearing people online... no one knows the person they're talking to is deaf.